Changing Woman

Janine Canan

Scars Publications and Design

Changing Woman

Janine Canan

ISBN# 1-891470-21-3

Scars Publications and Design
ccandd96@aol.com   http://www.yotko.com/scars
printed in the United States of America
with assistance from Freedom and Strength Printers

Acknowledgments

Some of these poems were first published in the chapbooks *Love, Enter* (Ope Bone Press, Port Angeles WA, 1998), and *Goddess Poems* (Sagitarrius Press, Por Townsend WA, 1997, letterpress). "And I Release You" was published as a letterpres keep-sake (Oyez Press, Berkeley CA, 1998). Several poems were published with pho tographs by Elyse Ebright as a set of greeting cards (Port Townsend, 1997). Sever; poems were published as broadsides: "And I Release You", with monoprints b Elizabeth Ingraham; "The Goddesses", with drawing by Molly Sokolow; an "Revelations". Alma Villanueva has quoted "The Handle" as the frontispiece to he poetry collection *Vida* (Bilingual Press, Tempe AZ, 2000), and Lucia Birnbaum ha quoted from "Oh, Kali" in her *Godmothers-African Origins*. Watercolor paintings b Dianne Baumunck were inspired by "Forest Temple".

Thankful acknowledgment to the editors who included some of these poems i their anthologies: *American Poets Say Goodbye to the Twentieth Century by Andr Codrescu* (4 Walls 8 Windows, New York NY, 1996); *Collected Poems: Marrowstor Poets and Friends* by Pat Britt and Gwen Moore (Turtle Press, Marrowstone WA 1995); *Contemporary Authors*, edited by Joyce Nakamura, The Gale Grou; Farmington Hills MI, 1999; *The Divine Feminine: Exploring the Feminine Face God Around the World* by Andrew Harvey and Anne Baring (Conari Press, Berkele CA, 1996); *From the Realm of the Ancestors: Essays in Honor of Marija Gimbutas* b Joan Marler (Knowledge, Ideas & Trends, Manchester CT, 1997); *Get Well Wishe Prayers and Poems to Wish You Well* by June Cotner (Harper, San Francisco CA, 200C

Hard Love: Writings on Intimacy and Violence by Elizabeth Clamen (Queen of Swords, Eugene OR, 1996); *Heal Your Soul, Heal the World: Prayers and Poems to Comfort, Inspire and Connect Humanity* by June Cotner (Andrews McMeel, Kansas City MO, 1998); *Her Words* by Burleigh Muten (Shambhala, Boston MA, 1999); *It's All The Rage! Poems About Suicide and Its Alternative* by Candace Hall (Andrew Mountain Press, Hartford CT, 1997); *Home to Ourselves: Women's Life Journeys to Goddess Honoring* by Nicole Desjeunes and Bonnita Lynn, Dolphin Press, Albuquerque NM, 1999; *The Largeness the Small is Capable Of,* by Crag Hill (SCORE Publications, Pullman WA, 1999). *Least Loved Beasts of the Really Wild West: A Tribute* by Terril and Yvette Shorb (Native West Press, Prescott AZ, 1997); *Mirrors of Silver, Mirrors of Lead: Stories by Women* by Georgianna Bowley (Aporia, New Brunswick NJ, 1990); *Prayers to Protest: Poems that Center and Bless Us* by Jennifer Bosveld (Pudding House, Johnstown OH, 1997); *Sirius Verse* by Bradley Strahan and Shirley Sullivan (Black Dog Press, Church Falls VA, 1998); *Return of the Goddess, 2000 Engagement Calendar* by Burleigh Muten, Stewart, Tabori, Chang, New York NY, 1999; *A Watch of Angels: Violetta Books 1996 Poetry Anthology* by Kathleen Gilbert (Violetta Books, Springfield MA, 1996); *We'Moon '99: Gaia Rhythms for Womyn* and *We'moon '98: Wise Womyn Ways,* edited by Bethroot Gwynn, and *We'moon '94 Gaia Calendar,* edited by Musawa (Mother Tongue Ink, Estacada OR, 1998); and *We Speak for Peace* by Ruth Jacobs (Knowledge, Ideas & Trends, Manchester CT, 1993).

Thankful acknowledgment to the editors who published earlier versions of these poems in the journals: *The Acorn, Along the Path, Alternative Harmonies, Aporia, Arnazella, The Aurorean, The Bloomsbury Review, Caprice, Colorado North Review, Color Wheel, Convolvulus, Crone Chronicles, Daughters of Nyx, Exquisite Corpse, Friendly Woman, The Gentle Survivalist, Goddessing, Heart & Wings, The Higher Source, It's About Time, Kalliope, Kavindra, The Kerf, The Kore, The Laureate Letter, Luna, Matriarch's Way, Minotaur, Of The People, Open Bone Review, Phoenix Rising, Poetalk, Poetry: USA, Potato Eyes, The Port Townsend Leader, Pudding Magazine, Saraswati, Sonoma Mandala, Surprise Me, Talking Raven, The Temple, Tight, West Wind Review, A Wise Woman's Garden,* and *Writer's Gazette.*

Thank yous also to radio producers Jane Heaven and Joan Marler, who recorded many of these poems on *Magic in the Air* and *Brainstorm,* respectively, at KPFA Pacifica Radio in Berkeley, 1991. Special thanks to the friends who read this manuscript with loving care: Susan Hahn, Patricia Laferriere, Peggy Lynne, Burleigh Muten, David Taylor and Alma Luz Villanueva. To Michael Ballen for his angelic help with the computer, and Justine Shapiro for her fresh gust of encouragement. Above all I offer my thanks to my friend Kris Brandenburger for her passionate, inspired and steadfast attention to the complex unfolding of this collection over many years.

Cover painting, *Gray Line with Black, Blue and Yellow* by Georgia O'Keeffe, courtesy of The Houston Museum. Graphic designs adapted from neolithic artworks in Marija Gimbutas' *The Language of the Goddess* (Harper & Row, 1989) and *The Civilization of the Goddess* (Harper San Francisco, 1991).

Poetry Books by Janine Canan

Of Your Seed (Oyez, Berkeley CA, 1977)

Who Buried the Breast of Dreams (Emily Dickinson, Berkeley CA, 1981)

Daughter (Emily Dickinson, Berkeley CA, 1981)

Shapes of Self (Emily Dickinson, Berkeley CA, 1982)

Her Magnificent Body, New & Selected Poems (Manroot, San Francisco CA, 1986)

She Rises like the Sun: Invocations of the Goddess by Contemporary American Women Poets, Editor (The Crossing, Freedom CA, 1989)

Goddess Poems (Sagittarius, Port Townsend WA, 1997, letterpress)

Love, Enter (Open Bone, Port Angeles WA, 1998)

Star in My Forehead: Selected Poems by Else Lasker-Schüler, Translator (Holy Cow!, Duluth MN, 2000)

The Rhyme of the Ag-ed Mariness: Last Poems of Lynn Lonidier, Editor (Station Hill, Barrytown NY, 2000)

Preface

All things alter ceaselessly, even the Unalterable. Though ineffable in potency the Divine Feminine proliferates into countless forms, manifesting in the reality of every being, every situation, every breath.

The poet lives to celebrate the glories of these phenomena. But without a valor of compassion and an allegiance to love no poetic mind can dissolve the webs and vortexes of desire's kingdom and reveal the transcendent in the mundane.

Here are gathered, with tenderness and pride, the records of one poet's penetrating journey through the metamorphic realms of bewilderment and bliss. Honor her trophies.

James Broughton

Janine Canan

Contents

To Iris Murdoch,

in immortal memory

Introduction to the Poet

The poet can reach where the sun cannot.

— Hindu Proverb

Introduction to the Poet

At the zenith of Patriarchy's Five Thousand Years War, on the second Day of the Dead when the spirits of dead children return among the living, at high noon—I was born. I slid from my mother's anesthetized womb into Saint Vincent's hospital in the City of the Queen of Angels—the city where my great-grandmother, my grandmother and my mother had entered before me. The welcoming hands of a white-coifed nun tucked me into a niche in her long black gown, that rustled with the untold feminine mysteries of the millennia.

Soon afterward my father drove us, in a little maroon Lincoln, home to an orange grove south of the City. It was November, 1942, and the oranges were still green. My mother, Mary, a dreamy young beauty who had grown up nurturing herself on books, soon had me propped beside her as she read rhymes out of *My Little Book House*. This twelve volume collection of literary marvels gathered by Olive Beaupré Miller was my earliest introduction to poetry. Among its beautifully illustrated pages I met Mother Goose, Hans Anderson, William Shakespeare, Elizabeth Browning, John Keats, Christina Rossetti, Alfred Tennyson and others. From it, Mother read me the ancient songs of India, Africa, Europe and America. Her lovely alto voice filled the room with lullabies, as orange blossoms flooded our creamy farmhouse with their sweet pungent fragrance. The doors stood open on the land of Beauty.

When I was two, we moved into Los Angeles, so Father could be nearer his restaurant, the Wichstand. My first sister was born. Our new home was a three-story white house built into a hill that overlooked the sprawling palm-lined city. On Palmero Street massive catalpa trees shed their large dark pods along the sidewalk. In the backyard a towering avocado with lanky leaves and a sturdy magnolia with huge perfumy white flowers thrived alongside numerous fruit trees—peaches, apricots, pomegranates, figs, lemons, limes, kumquats and loquats. Masses of magenta bougainvillea blooms scampered up the wall to my bedroom.

Around the house flowerbeds brimmed with roses and begonias. Pink, white and lavender geraniums, tangled with ivy, crawled down the hillside. At night the lights of the city crowded into the boughs of the trees.

For me, my sisters Dianne and Michele, and herself, Mother arranged all kinds of lessons in the arts. I began with tap dance, piano, and ballet; followed by violin, marimba, oil painting, and flamenco dance; later on ballroom and modern dance, German (Mother was learning German *Lieder*), and—at last—the harp.

> One Christmas I woke up early and crept downstairs to leave my presents, before everyone else awoke—down the rose wool stairs, down the beige stairs onto cold linoleum floor. Rounding the corner, my eyes flew to *the harp*—tall regal golden lover! I circled round, I breathed on her, and where I touched, her strings resounded. *(Her Magnificent Body,* "Her Strings")

On holidays we all performed for one another—even my father joined in, playing the only piece he remembered from piano lessons for which he had saved as a teen during the hard years of the Great Depression.

I loved school, and had many devoted teachers and good school friends. In first grade we all danced around the maypole, floating up and down on long crepe paper streamers. We memorized Longfellow's "The Children's Hour". In fourth grade, Helen Hum introduced us to the heartwarming Laura Ingalls Wilder books; hugging us against her big bosom, she encouraged us to paint with lots of color. The next year we performed Louisa May Alcott's *Little Women*—I as the narrator. From a neighbor I inherited a whole collection of riveting Nancy Drew mysteries. And for my twelfth birthday, Mother took me to the opera and I was swept into the romantic world of *La Bohème*. The next year a crush on a teacher inspired my first love poem. At home, in Mother's library of novels, poetry, history and psychology, I discovered the Bronte sisters; curling myself into a generously stuffed aquamarine chair next to the Quan Yin lamp I immersed myself in the passionate saga of *Jane Eyre*.

The summer before high school, I rushed to take American Literature. In the large cool rooms of the high-ceilinged Los Angeles Public Library, I poured over piles of books on the poetry of Thomas Stearns Eliot, and fell in love with my first Poet. The next year my high school French teacher—a short intense woman with large piercing brown eyes, ultra-high heels and oily black braid woven round her head in a great corona—introduced me to the mysteries of André Gide. Joyfully, I joined the Dorsey High School Chorus and poured myself into Bach. On a Mariners' sailing trip under the stars, I threw myself into a dramatic rendition of *King Lear* while my mates nodded off into sleep. And for graduation my parents gave me, to my extreme delight, *The Poems of Emily Dickinson* in three volumes including all variant manuscripts, published for the first time that year by Harvard.

At seventeen I entered Stanford University, intending to become a psychiatrist, but soon changed my major to French. At Stanford I luxuriated in a fabulous classical education, enjoying Georges Lemaitre's whimsical presentations in Sartre and Existentialism; Frederick Spiegelberg's awesome Religions of the World, which included a lesson in the use of Himalayan ghost traps; and young Theodore Roszak's elegant Introduction to Western Civilization. By then playing harp in the Stanford Orchestra, and starting to learn harpsichord, I often carried under my arm an increasingly tattered volume of collected poems by e. e. cummings, to whom I had been introduced by my fiancé's mother, Molly.

Michael Canan, a witty, politically inclined Stanford economics student, insisted we go to Berkeley for graduate school after our wedding. There I soon became absorbed into the Anti-War Movement that was rapidly gaining momentum by 1963. Supposedly studying German literature so I could read the mystical poetry of Rilke, more and more I was caught up in the gathering maelstrom of Flower Consciousness. Many hours were spent at rousing campus demonstrations against racism and The War. Standing in Cody's Books on Telegraph Avenue, I read every new poetry edition that arrived on the shelf— from Robert Duncan's rhythmic *Opening of the Field*, to Michael McClure's mysterious *Dark Brown*. In the joyous Summer of 1965, an unforgettable Berkeley Poetry Conference presented one-eyed Creeley, howling Ginsberg, raging Le Roi Jones; humongous drunken bear Olson, lively lisping Levertov in striped tee-shirt, ascetic Snyder with goatee, and Duncan overpowered by incessant visions. A yogi arrived from India proclaiming Berkeley "the heartbeat of the world".

In the Sixties the Bay Area throbbed with poetry, effervesced with poetry, *was* poetry. Robert Duncan was often seen flying down Telegraph Avenue in his magic cape. Julia Vinograd, dressed in black and yellow robe and cap, limped into cafes peddling booklets of poems for a dollar. At the Berkeley Community Theater Janis Joplin, in her sexy short black dress, belted out cosmic lyrics to the accompaniment of Big Brother and the Holding Company; while Ram Dass pontificated afterwards. In San Francisco Glenn Gould hovered over his piano, humming indecipherable chants. At the Jazz Workshop Coltrane poured out his heart through his sublime saxophone. Ali Akbar Khan and Ravi Shankar arrived in the Berkeley Amphitheater with their soulful sarod and sitar. And at the Golden Gate Park Love-In, Allen Ginsberg sang of the fall of America, transcendently stoned—but by then I was too in-love with my Rilke professor to make the scene.

Eventually I took an illuminating poetry workshop with Canadian poet Peter Dale Scott, began to write seriously, publish poetry, and teach workshops myself. In 1971, the University of California opened its new Art Museum, and hoards of poets came to sing in celebration. I too read a few poems, followed by William Everson and Judy Grahn—who recited her stunning *Common Woman* poems. The Women's Movement was unfolding. The tender and explosive secrets of Alta, Griffin and Grahn appeared in the bookstores in stapled editions.

As the Sixties slowly began to wind down, I remembered my unrealized plan, harbored since I was thirteen, of becoming a psychiatrist. Thanks to the scholarships and loans I received, I was able to attend New York University School of Medicine from 1972 to 1976. During those years, as soon as I got back to my studio apartment after a long day at the hospital, I poured myself a glass of wine and composed poems on an old Royal typewriter, stationed on a piece of plywood balanced on orange crates salvaged from the street. Or I let myself become absorbed by the rich Anglo poetry of Auden and Levertov, which particularly appealed to me then. In New York I had the great pleasure of hearing many remarkable poets—Muriel Rukeyser, Denise Levertov, Adrienne Rich, Stephen Spender. At Lincoln Center I worshipped at the musical altars of Menuhin, Diskau, Brendel.

But I was homesick, longing to feel the heartwarming beams of California again. And so in 1976 I returned to Berkeley for a psychoanalytically/oriented residency at Herrick Hospital. My friend Carolyn Verlinden introduced my poetry to Robert Hawley, editor and publisher of Oyez, a small Berkeley press publishing poetry by Duncan, Levertov, Everson and others. In the late Seventies, Robert published my first chapbook, *Of Your Seed*, a "seed" collection of lyric and dramatic portraits. In those years I was reading and loving Sherwood Anderson's *Winesburg, Ohio*, John Berryman's *Dream Songs*, and Adrienne Rich's *Twenty-One Love Poems*. I joined a poetry group with Josephine Miles, who amazed me with her ability to mend almost anything made of words. Later on I took a workshop on Revising the Poem with Carolyn Kizer, *grande dame* of American poetry, and learned to dismantle and rebuild a poem like an automobile engine.

In 1981 I established Emily Dickinson Press, and soon published my next three books: *Who Buried the Breast of Dreams, Daughter,* and *Shapes of Self*—th latter a collection of eighty kaleidoscopic prose-poetic glimpses of the soul. Now the poems were coming—while walking, driving, swimming, listening to music, reflecting and meditating—as if out of my own body, out of the fabric of nature Herself, with a voice that increasingly knew what She had to say. It was a lush period for the emergence of women's writing. In 1982 Stanford University invited 15 women poets, including Josephine Miles, Denise Levertov, Carolyn Kizer, Judy Grahn, Audre Lorde and Alma Villanueva, to join in their festive and widely attended Conference on Women and Poetry.

Although powerful writing by women was flourishing by the Eighties, another kind of poetry was emerging which I did not like—a kind of false poem, well-crafted, highly polished, but lacking in authentic heart and soul. This *persona poem*, as I call it, speaks from the superficial layers of the personality, substituting the little defending and maneuvering ego for the infinitely creative Self, which is the true subject of poetry. Persona poetry expresses the anonymous voice of society, tends to be flat and sound alike; indeed, many American literary journals of this period can be read as if written by one person (or ghost?). This pointless anti-poetry is the enemy of truth and beauty—toward which any true poet endlessly strives. Today, in the final moments of the West's Second Millennium, this post-modern body of so-called poetry, identity-less child of an ever more materialistic and amoral society, rots in its terminal meditation on the emptiness of the ego. To these writers, poetry is a sport.

Real poetry is revelation! It reveals the complex unity, both horrendous and sublime, of our human experience. Real art is pure essence of human being. It illumines the wholiness and sacredness of life. Poetry is the language not of society and certainly not of the ego; in its highest form it is the language of the Gods. This divine language is one the poet is forever in the process of learning. For poetry is not mere words; it is something that comes and goes in words. For a real poet, the tongue is holy. Is this, perhaps, why many ancient Gods—the Balinese Rangda, the Indian Kali, the Aztec Sun God—are portrayed with enormous lengthy protruding tongues? Poetry is an extra-ordinary form of communication, one of the most condensed means of transmitting information that exists. And in the end, it is poetry that writes the real, the lasting human document. There is an old Hindu proverb which states, *The poet can reach where the sun cannot.* A real poet is a seer who speaks beyond time, soul to soul—a priest who brings us in direct contact with the ultimate and guides us to joyful acceptance. Real poetry is a spiritual practice for both writer and reader, offering and receiving the totality of the soul. Art is play, it is politics, it is many things, but above all it is praise, a form of worship. And what makes art great is the poet's love for the subject. "Writing is an act of love—if it isn't that, it is handwriting,"

Cocteau put it wittily.

"Song seems somehow the very central essence of us," Carlyle once said. Poetry is "the very breath of all friendliness," wrote Thoreau. It is "the joy of language," claimed Stevens. *Impossible* pain and joy," added Weil. "A moment's monument," said Shelley; "a concentration...of a very great number of experiences," said Eliot; "the inner life of a culture," said Jong. "A poet will accidentally define his time," Crane believed, "simply by reacting honestly and to the full extent of his sensibilities to the states of passion, experience and rumination that fate forces on him, first-hand." "Art is the harmonious coalescence of all learning," a Tibetan lama has said. "Art is a way of recognizing oneself," says French sculptor Louise Bourgeois. Writer Samuel Beckett aptly suggested that the heart of an onion or a cauliflower might make a more appropriate tribute to poetic labor than the crown of bay. —For art, all art, is whatever is done with ever deepening care in service to the Source. Surrendering to the Gods, the poet merely tunes in—the music is always playing.

In the Eighties, discouraged by much contemporary poetry, when not occupied with the patients in my psychiatric practice, I found myself turning more and more to the divine Greek poet Sappho, the Chinese lyric poet Tu Fu, the English love poet Shakespeare, the ecstatic American poet Emily Dickinson, and to the ancient *Upanishads* of India—for wisdom, passion and beauty. During that decade I fell madly in love with the wildly rich and abundant novels of Iris Murdoch—novels that plumb the depths of human passions. Her creative genius became for many years my teacher and my guide. In 1984 I had the great honor of meeting her. Around this time I was also introduced to Robert Duncan by my friend, the poet Lynn Lonidier; as well as to Paul Mariah, the editor of Manroot Press in San Francisco (publisher of Lonidier, Broughton, Gunn, Cocteau and others). Paul appreciated, above all, the elegiac aspect of my work, and published in 1986 my next book, *Her Magnificent Body: New & Selected Poems.*

In 1987 I suddenly became stunningly aware of the powerful return of the Goddess. While viewing a beautifully inspired collection of Goddess artwork at a perinatal psychology conference, I became consumed with the task of gathering the contemporary poetry manifesting Her. In a whirlwind I edited the anthology, *She Rises like the Sun: Invocations of the Goddess by Contemporary American Women Poets,* published by The Crossing Press in 1989. *She Rises like the Sun* offered a rich assortment of metaphysically revolutionary, post-patriarchal poems by 29 poets, including Angelou, Di Prima, Grahn, Griffin, Harjo, Hogan, Levertov, Lorde, Morgan, Piercy, Sarton, Shange, Villanueva, Vinograd and Wakoski.

The same year that *She Rises like the Sun* came out, San Francisco experienced the most severe earthquake it had experienced since the turn of the century. Freeways came down and hills crumbled. In my own life, on the most personal of levels, an inner earthquake was taking place which dissolved a deeply valued relationship, and levered me out of my beloved Berkeley into the world at large. Feeling devastated, I fled to Asia—first to Bali, then on to India, where I spent profoundly enlightening time with my Vedanta teacher, Swami Dayananda, at his ashram. From India I flew to Paris, France, where I remained for the rest of the year, to take the healing waters of beauty in the city of *Notre Dame*. And from Paris I rode the train to Thalheim, Germany, to visit one of the living Divine Mothers of the world, Mother Meera.

When I returned to America—ambivalently—it was in the wooded Pacific Northwest, in the northwesternmost corner of the United States, in a small town on a tiny peninsula near the Canadian border, that I decided to settle. "Welcome to the end of the road," my dear eighty-year-old friend James Broughton greeted me, chuckling. Between 1992 and 1998, I lived on the Juan de Fuca Strait with my beloved Samoyed dogs Sophia and Devi, my cat Marianne, the countless birds that nested around my house, the magnificent guardian cedars and firs, the talkative waters of the nearby strait, the stones with their fabulous stories strewn over the sands, and overhead the exultant ever-changing light-bringing sky.

The poems in this collection, *Changing Woman,* were written between 1986 and 1999. They recount my spiritual journey during these years: my political perceptions as a woman, my personal sorrows and joys, and the healing revelations that have taken place in California, Asia and Europe; in meetings with great souls—Ammachi, Mother Meera, Pir Vilayat, Sri Ma, Mother Teresa; and mostly on the singing shores of Port Townsend. In paintings, sculptures and dances; stories, confessions, sermonettes and prayers; in fits and outpourings, with pleas and caresses, amidst weeping and laughing, they chant my changes, the changes of women throughout the world, and the changes of the Divine One Herself. May this diary of my heart bring you joy and solace, unexpected thoughts, the full range of your own emotions, soaring visions, and revelations that change your mind and open your heart. I offer these poems—each one "a phial of my blood", as Picasso once said of his art—at the feet of the Great Mother of us all: she who ever changing remains the same.

Janine Canan

Janine Canan

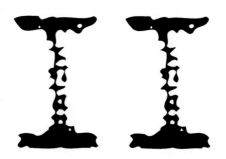

In The Country
of War

Janine Canan

Janine Canan

In the Country of War

Once the world was wild.
Mother drenched her darling boy in milk and honey.
He built the house, the road, the car—and woman
made their home, their conversation during the long journey.
Now he, for millennia worshipped with flowers and fire,
must retreat in silence, smoke and shame.
He has slain the breathing trees, stolen the friendly land,
raped the knowing women.
He poisons rivers, seas and skies; the roaming animals,
the sensing plants, his own land, his own kin.
He gives his sons weapons and teaches them to kill.
He imagines he is bigger than God.

*

In the Country of War the sky is always black.
The President paints on more black.
A mother offers her babe to the violencevision.
A father gives his son a full set of killer toys.
Men construct machines that harm all life.
Schoolboys draw war missiles
(a nation of bombs has no money for books).
Girls, harrassed, go to empowerment class.
The citizens are building up!
The forests felled, waters fouled, air polluted—
the embryos retreat.
Breasts multiply in revolt!

*

The trees rustle, *We are dying.*
The mountains moan, *Stripped, we have no snow.*
And still, mad men strive for more!
On an arid mountain peak
the Ancients throw open their gate:
Younger brother has robbed the Mother—
She who is fertility
and intelligence,
whose blood is made of gold.
The world does not have to end,
but it will end,
unless he understands.

*

To exist, to understand, to be happy—to feel loved
is all that humans want.
No one can be happy living in an Empire of Greed.
Insomnia, infertility, chronic pain, incessant weeping
and complaining, panic and heart-break
are signs of empire's fall.
Long black limousines arrive for the funeral.
To find Her, dig deep into Earth's memory.
Bathe Her, no bigger than your hand,
in your own tears.
Adorn Her—the Enduring Woman—
with your white lily, pink lotus, scarlet rose.

*

In the room the women come and go
talking not of Michelangelo but of Brassempouy,
hers the first face lifted from mud! Of Grimaldi,
Dordogne, Laussel with crescent and belly,
of Willendorf, Dolni Vestonice, Los Angeles and Malta—
She of Africa, Asia, America, Europe, beyond the world and worlds.
In the room where fluorescent light bulbs squeal

the women come and go talking of Her of amber, bone and ivory,
Her to whom Enheduanna chanted thousands of years ago,
She who perched upon the caves hundreds of thousands of years,
whose body is the earth and sky, Creation's ever changing dream.
Oh Mother Dawning, the women cry, *welcome, long-awaited Belonging.*

*

Why choose death?
In this night with no moonlight,
flashlight or candle,
dive in the darkness inside Her.
She who is every memory and possibility,
who is every grace and loss—
do you understand?—
She who is You
will change your mind.
In the center of your Self is the Mother.
Where the Mother is, is your Self.
Call Her—Mata, Tara, Mary—and it's dawn!

*

One day man and woman will kiss,
phallus will bow and enter
the narrow moist passageway,
offering his inmost sweetness
upon her crimson altar.
Bounding forth from her hidden cave,
she will pull him into her pounding heart
that swells to Creation's brilliant rim
and spills into the stars.
From every egg the Goddess grows.
One day man will play his bass
and woman sing.

*

She is a snake, She is a bird.
She is the Earth opening her million petals.
She is the birth of conscious life.
She is the glacier that comes and goes,
the cycling essence, the tiniest seed.
She disappears in metal armor and arrogant power,
and reappears in golden life.
She is the kiss, the discovery, the difficulty
that leads you on, stretching out her arms of loving light.
Her heart is within you.
She is life. She is beyond life.
She alone is.

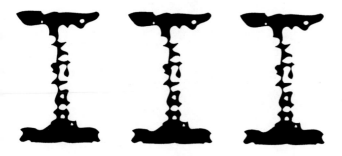

Fathers' Night

As a woman I have no country.
As a woman I want no country.
As a woman the whole world is my country.

—Virginia Woolf

End of the Masculine Age

Listening to the Male News,
seated in my male chair, feeling sore
since neither chair nor news fit me or any of my sex,
I look round my house where all the fixtures
are slightly high, and every surface exudes man's poison.
My gaze escapes the northern window to the waving trees,
who I realize are waving *Goodbye!*
The red, bronze and golden ground
that I—like the lion—love to lie upon,
is everywhere blackly paved.
All day long machines raid the silence,
smothering my sisters, the sweet voiced birds.

How did all this start—and why? I groan,
soon sickening on my own anger.
Don't I know that for some reason—A Mystery,
She desired, willed, ordained and made it so.
She must have wanted the clumsy brute
to seize and fire and form Her world,
though now he mainly infuriates it.
Oh Great Mother, am I supposed to feel thankful?
I know this is hubris, but can't help wondering,
has Infinite She gone too far?
Has the roiling world, like a peppery stew
left boiling on the stove, escaped Her supreme attention?

Or is all this commotion just provocation?
I picture Her great flamenco in the sky, and in my staccato heart.
What awakening does She want with Her scorching glance?
Though I risk being called *a man-hater*
(what difference can that make at this late date—
a woman is never heard anyway),
I simply can't see the paltry kings ever surrendering.
Drunk on power, likely they will fight Her to a bloody end.
She will have to rectify the situation.
What worries me most is that I feel almost eager
for whatever devastation She in Her Awesome
chooses to right the wild imbalance.

Out of Business

Mrs. Bentley strides into the dressing room
and feels my breasts, lifting them up.
"Bring the next size!" she calls, receding
into nightgowns, leotards and ballet shoes.

At a chamber concert, accompanied by the doctor
with the best bedside manner in town
(a mystery writer whose *nom de plume*
no one knows), Mrs. Bentley is radiant.

Now blank strangers ask what kind of bras
I am looking for. —Where is Mrs. Bentley?
A street where dope pushers, spies and assassins traffic
is no place for a woman's store.

The lovely young dancers are gone,
and Bentley's has gone out of business.
Now who will tend young breasts
during patriarchy's long darkening night?

When Father Dies

When Father dies, his hair gone white,
no more time to rinse it bright,
shave his cheek, dress so neat,
thin all skin, and bones won't stand.

When Father dies, too tired to walk,
wheelchair now and hospital bed,
no business calls, no signing checks
or driving shiny Cadillacs.

When Father dies, no breath
in his lungs, no air in his blood,
no wish to eat, his feet so big,
his heart won't pump.

When Father dies, his voice so soft,
children gone away, astray,
no more demands to come home,
no more patriotic tirades.

When Father dies, no gifts or loans
or firm advice, no boat rides
or fast drives, no Mother saying
He's so stubborn, men are all that way.

When Father dies, they come and take it
all away, everything he worked for,
self-made man, all the money
he made buying and selling land.

When Father dies, no more family,
no more American dream,
developing desert and mountain and shoreline,
the bombs piled high.

When Father dies, poor baby,
poor thing, he mostly sleeps
or wakes in pain, no more time
to be anxious or kind.

You have to come, you have to go,
Old Father says,
no more breath, no more life,
no more avoiding death, the void.

When Father dies, the sky is clear,
the sky is cold, the sun is bright
and oh so slight,
the mountains snowy white.

When Father dies, no one
to open the window,
no one to turn out the light
for the little girl who cries and cries.

When Father dies, he says *Goodbye,*
following his father and mother,
his sister and brother,
leaving his body, his home.

When Father dies, he no longer cares
about his heirs, busy with dying,
accepting and fighting, remembering
and forgetting his failures and sins.

When Father dies, he smiles so sweetly,
what agonized eyes,
enjoying and suffering,
learning to live with his fears.

When Father dies, his loved ones
are praying for courage and light
as he turns to water, to air, to fire,
he sees with wide open eyes.....

Dear Sister

To Dianne Burford

Many years have passed—
you working your fate in the distant forest,
I in the city, wading a congested maze
weighted by outrage and fear,
dazed by the excess, cruelty, horror.

Today I drove to the music store
that towers over America, setting
our rhythms, arranging our actions,
sending human signals over the technological chain—
to hear what your favorite singer, Joni, had to say:

Money is the road to justice.
Preachers preaching love like vengeance,
lawyers teaching anyone can sue;
thieves and financiers parade, while bombs
and laws proliferate—there's evil in this land.

In the Sixties, long hair falling
over your knees, folded in lotus position,
your ears opened to her song's wistful purity.
Now she wails across the toxic sky:
Nothing savored long enough to understand.

Foresightful Sister, no wonder you wanted to exit
this ditch of corruption and pain.
High in your mountains, where breezes whistle
and a thousand birds converse, do you hear
the chain-saws tearing the world down.

Mexican Food

Do you know that Mexican food—*tacos, tostados, enchiladas colorados y verdes*—can heal all our wounds? In the smog and glamour-filled deserts of *Los Angeles,* Mexican food was my mother. As I rode the bus to Lindy's Delicatessen in Beverly Hills for relief as needed, mooned over Oscar Levant's outpatient appearances on television, where his leaden fingers stumbled wittily over the keys of the twentieth century, and heeded the tender angry lyrics of Kenneth Patchen wept to jazz in the Venice coffee-house-dark of the crinoline-skirted fifties—it was Mexican food that taught me enduring goodness.

And so I believe that even today Mexican food can heal the wounds of the world, but reserve this knowledge for eccentric moral explorers—or Mexican food will become as expensive as French; Mexican restaurant owners will require liability insurance to protect themselves from litigious consumers whose white-washed shirts are stained by dribbling *salsa;* and when the personal injury profiteers discover *burning tongue,* and the gullible California jurors return to the courtroom with their verdict *Guilty,* insurance for Mexican restaurants will triple, driving their owners back to *Mejico* bankrupt, you can con on that, America!

But I know that Mexican food can heal all the wounds of the world, the soul of the world lies in a *Casa de Eva* flauta, and all happiness in the perfect *Margarita* with foam, *La Tertulia's* bread pudding with cheese, and creamy *atillas!* Do not pass it on, do not print up flyers, do not run ads in magazines, on television, or to millions of over-burdened liberals in the mail. Do not ask for donations to save poor downtrodden Mexican cooks. Mexican restaurants do not need loans to expand, computerized cash registers, Macs to reformat their menus; more business, more income, more taxes, more bombs, more hate and more greed!

For I know there is a smile in *Baja California* on the face of a Mexican family drinking tequila and eating *tortillas y frijoles*—as Steinbeck wrote in *Tortilla Flat,* "What more you want?"—or boiling lobsters by the sea. And that everywhere in Mexico—midst corruption, killing, exploitation and thievery—there something good to eat. Even in New Mexico are varieties of *chiles* sufficient to fill a thesaurus—*jalapeños, serranos, anjos*—colors of red that will sear your heart with a happiness that spreads like the wide open sky: clear air, scent of sage, warm *tortillas,* and chile, chile, chile!

Yes, I know that Mexican food can save the world but do not tell, or I would be held responsible for America's suffering—for giving this advice free. Insure me, and I might tell you about some of my deepest experiences with Mexican food—if it weren't that tying me up in a lawsuit for ten years with chess-playing lawyers, blood-red nail-polished private investigators and debauched inquisitors obsessed with sex, interferes with eating enough of that Goddess-given Mexican food, *olé! Chiles rellenos, quesadillas, huevos rancheros, menudo* chicken *mole, chocolate mejicano, sopapillas* with honey!

And still I know that Mexican food is the road to salvation. Any crisis, any stab in the heart or even the back can be ameliorated by real hot fresh *salsa* chicken rolled in corn *tortillas,* refried beans, *Dos Equis* dark (don't sue me *Carta Blanca!*), or a pitcher of *Margaritas* unfrozen! Oh, *guacamole* with *tostaditas!* In California, in New Mexico, in the *Yucatan,* there lies the treasure of youth, of joy, the seed of an ecstasy that grows out over the direst conditions, the dreariest human boredom, the most abysmal human stupidity, and I know, know that Mexican food can cure all the wounds of the world.

And so when I die, I would like to be buried in Mexican food served in a family restaurant unincorporated, or mulched at the foot of a gigantic chile plant leafy and green, giving vitamin C-rich *chiles* to feed our children of the future. Fed in the eternally youthful *be here now, make love not war,* permissive and nutritional Doctor Spock-Adele Davis-Linus Pauling Sixties manner even in *Amerika*—a smile will return to their innocent faces, hope to their eyes gleaming once again with pleasure, a red *chile* to their mouths, a white and a blue corn *tortilla* to their hands! For I know Mexican food can cure the agony of our times.

Though many will cry, *All Mexican food tastes alike!*—if there is one thing I can absolutely promise, it is that Mexican food is never the same. Now exquisitely scalloped *tortillas* flapping from hand to hand over a child at play on the sand—now micro-waved taco-pasted processed American cheese at *Nevada* gambling casino where *desperados* use nuclear bombs for dice. Tonight at my table a happy surprise: *Enchiladas Chihuahueñas* with shredded beef bathed in crimson sauce with a dollop of radiant cream! This I drink with my cheery California red wine—for once we were *Mejica* and will be again. *Amigos,* Mexican food's tangible living delight will resurrect the crucified body of our times.

What Woman Wants

First woman does womanly things,
then she does what man does (even better).
But as she pushes against his brutal metal,
the more she wants to be woman,
enjoying the world as it is.

Woman wants to touch the leaf,
speak in growing ripples,
blushing with joy at her thoughts
that come from so far away—
a miracle is what woman wants.

Woman wants to plant the seed,
see the dream, sink into sleep.
To breathe!—joy the song
she hums as she walks in love,
tuned to the Goddess in everyone.

So come to woman, and let us begin again—
stars blazing the void with light.
Then in the ceaseless flow,
as one moment dissolves in the next,
you will find your heart's joy.

Tumbling Back to Earth

I remember that journey back into the body,
down corridors occupied by phantoms,
tubes in every orifice rushing air and water
to save your life.

I remember that writhing to be free
as you twist against restraints, and groaning fail;
for once I too could not bear life's pain,
gulped every pill and nearly expired.

And I remember that great surge of Life,
reclaiming me afterward in its dharmic service.
Squirming and grimacing, you still don't understand—
Why am I here? you ask.

Soon you'll remember—first the guilt,
then the laughter. Turning over,
you resemble one of Rubens' rosy angels
tumbling back to Earth—and I embrace you.

The Masseuse

To JM

My masseuse has discovered she is angry
with her mother for not protecting her.

Against your father's rage? I ask. She lifts her face
through the smoke of scented candles. No, sex.

I sob into the white sheet as her hands,
apologetic and smooth, begin to search.

And those other hands, large, rough—what did they do,
so now she feels a stranger to herself?

Shell earrings, blond curls tumble over her shoulder
as she reaches for my pain—pressing—rubbing—pulling,

triumphing over those brutal hands,
that mauled in the darkness of sheets and muffled cries.

Floating over my body, as I fearlessly receive her love,
her hands grasp the life of the soul.

The Passage

To Robbie Lamming

This suffering,
this ritual sorrow of woman—
by adding yours to mine,
do I lessen our pain?

Outside the airplane
cobbled clouds pave the sky.
Oh, where are we going?
This violent movie on the screen—
muscles, guns, shouting—
is this entertainment for hell?

The world is whole, yet broken
minds stutter and rave.
Again! the tyrant mocks.
His story, however, is ending.
A new song soars—burning, dazzling.
And softly falls like snow.

Nesting a moment,
suddenly it flies free.
Clouds part, revealing
rivers widening to the sea,
vast forests of evergreen, and beings—are they
human?—of such astonishing grace.

Kate's Song

To Kate Wolf

She was the singer who sang her heart:
You must give yourself to love,
if love is what you're after.

Guitar in her arms, she sang her heart:
There's a wind blowing down the canyon.
so hot and dry the rocks turn red.

Through tears and laughter, she sang her heart:
Grandmother Earth, give me a rest,
I take my place with the Woman in the West.

Plutonium in her bones, She sang her heart to death.

Your Daughters

Mother, do you really prefer
your sons to us, your daughters?

It seems forever my sisters and I
have sought your shining gaze.

How much longer must we lug around
these boulders of our broken hearts.

Death, Great Friend

To Doris Fink

I

Does that box you're in hamper your return? Earth can't get to your bones. Much of you must have melted by now, risen in gas to join the minerals, that feed the grass, whose leaves give oxygen to the air. Someone breathes you. The wind carries you over the world. Through gaps in the atmosphere, a few of your molecules enter space. A long time ago you started coming here—for a long time you'll be returning.

You're gone now, and I talk to myself. You'd appreciate this conversation, but you can't hear it. Talking to the dead, talking to myself on this bright spring day, I seem to be afraid of death, and don't accept life either. Nothing changes, everything changes—like an old Chinese poem. You're fixed now, you're dissipated. Farewell, then. I know you'll return—in memory, or some new substance.

II

I don't go out to your grave.
I see it clearly:
The pretty little hill,
the weeping tree nearby,
thick green well-mown grass in the sun,
where you whirl in the air.

III

You picked up the pieces after your mother was demolished by Nazis—in Germany a factory manager, in America a woman led in and out of hospitals for drugs and shock. At twelve your father stroked and you were on your own. You worked your way through art school; and during the decade your husband became a surgeon, entertained yourself with babies, paints and jazz.

You raised your daughters, three beautiful girls, to be independent like you. And it's a good thing! For cancer took you in nine months at age forty-six. In your last hours, nestled like a newborn, you lifted your face to be kissed. *I want you to feel joy,* you exclaimed. Dear Friend, how will I ever get over the bitterness of human suffering?

IV

Our friendship continues to grow, as the years roll on past your death—as if your paintings were still being painted. In the early years representa tional scenes of mother and child. Watery flowers becoming more inward landscapes intestinal gaining in power. What would they have become—thi inward coming out to face the world. Your soul face, your real face.

Our friendship now is invisible, yet every day more substantial. I need you as never before—your point of view, immense common sense penetrat ing the fuss of obsession, your strong heart speaking out. The friends who are distant are the ones easiest to talk to anyhow. Like a conscience made of soft ness—a persistent kind of love.

V

This loss goes on and on. You're never coming back, and no one can replace you. I think of your epic dreams, in which the history of the twenti eth century unfolded. What was in the air as concrete to you as to me— intu itions exchanged without obstacle. You saw evil, eager to fight for good. You hounded me when I strayed in loneliness.

Pretty, dark-eyed, shining olive-rose skin blended with the landscapes o Galilee—your warm voice sharpened when something was wrong. What you liked made you laugh like a baby. Happiness, righteousness, clarity you invented, as you danced and drew. And then your ovaries, that made three glory eggs, revolted, generating meaningless cells, chaos, death. How this loss goes on and on. You're never coming back. And no one can replace you.

VI

You're nothing but a crushed flower, petals soft and frail; like the petalled velvety vulva you painted with my face looking out. Oh, those female faces we wore, looking on with horror. There's no hope for changing the world—giant organism chaotic, cruel, crushing in its cornucopious productions: moments of perfect inspiration followed by inevitable deflation.

Attachment brings pain, non-attachment the void; doing freely for others both joy and violent punishment. *Now you see what the world is like,* said Tolstoi. Non-world bathes psyche and nature like sunlight or silver mist, in these portraits of life—ungraspable souls hinted at on paper and canvas: our lone lives.

VII

Children flown to Los Angeles, New York; husband remarried; pictures gone from the walls; the house sold—no sign left of you. Only your voice, my Soul, keeps calling. You're permanent now, Friend who'll always be near me. You haven't changed a bit. Oh Death, Great Friend, what huge arms You have, vast enveloping wings. You spread them, and we fly—dark and shining blue to the sun.

Akhmatova

Akhmatova, the oriole is always grieving—
is she happy or sad?
Silver willow sliced to a stump.

She suddenly came out of that trance so common to us all,
and whispered in my ear (everybody spoke in whispers there):
"Can you describe this?"

Lyre that became a rattle.
Incinerating your poems,
you bellowed a shroud over Stalingrad.

And I said, "Yes, I can."
Then something like the shadow of a smile
crossed what had once been her face.

Today in Saint Petersburg the snow drips
off your bronze eyelids.
And the stars above—are they happy or sad?

Oh Century, My Century

For Andrei Codrescu & Laura Rosenthal

Oh Century, my Century, whence have you come?
Cows and sheep once blissfully grazed
on Mother's millennial mounds.
Rivers chatted, berries bounded
past the pistachios and fat red apples,
grasses fed the ovens with bread.
The village gathered round Her temple
womb that over-brimmed with life.
Red pots spun with sacred design.
Naked priestesses danced in gold,
coaxing their lyres into grateful song.

Then, my Trembling One, six thousand years ago
horsemen swarmed from distant barren steppes
upon the loved and fertile land
swinging their daggers, spears and swords.
Inventors of weapons and slavery,
who worshipped the torrid sun
and wore strings of glaring teeth,
they razed and raided, raped and smashed.
Crushing the law of Nature,
they established the law of Terror—
the patriarch buried his own family in a tomb.

Twentieth Century—no!
You were never a century of Christ,
that divine Child of the Mother,
who taught the sweet sovereignty of love.
Metal men nailed his holy body to a cross
and crucified his teaching.
Surrender succumbed to dominance,
tenderness to violence.
Generosity was devoured by greed,
innocence twisted to guilt,

and beauty—beauty mocked to shame.

Are you, my maddened Century, to be the last?
Today Bully Boy rides bulldozer, sub, airplane and missile
bearing ammunition to destroy all life.
Land, sea and sky are inseminated with a million poisons.
What has he not raped? —The ancient tribes,
woman, child, plant and beast.
Even the atom, seed of creation, bleeds lethal radiation.
Murderer of the breathing Earth!
Seated on his massive throne of guns
at his mechanical money altar, adoring his own power—
he chews the heart of God.

Oh my Battered Queen, once voluptuously green,
can you remember still those caves
dark and moist with mirth,
where hundreds of centuries past birth began?
Walking through the white salt forest,
we entered the inner womb of wonder.
We lit Her fire, and on Her crystal flesh
we rang Her bellowing chimes.
Then fine-footed huge-bellied beasts
romped across Her surging walls,
bringing forth ecstatic life.

Oh Century, my laborious Century!
Drop by drop, the bloodied columns thicken.
But our ancient fire glows still.
Now is the time to strike our truest chord!
Her vast heart pounds—Her waters plash.
And moaning, praying, She pushes us
down the narrowing canal
against the stiff crimson door.
Lips stretch open to the light.
Her moment arches—sweet red petals flutter.
Into Her garden a lark is descending....

Janine Canan

Before the Storm

Two orioles perch on a telephone wire
stretched over a grassy oleander field, whistling.
Nearby workers listen to songs on the radio.

The mountains bend close
to find out what the humans are up to.
Birdlings tumble into bursting yellow blooms.

A broad black bird sails down valley.
On the highest hill towers the temple
to the Lord the whole world bows down to—

except one woman, who pauses on the lower steps
surveying the landscape, and above her
the slow-moving darkening clouds.

Janine Canan

Radioactive

Chernobyl,
Eniwetok,
Hiroshima,
Jornada del Muerte,
Nagasaki,
Nevada,
Pakistan,
Palomares,
Rajastan,
Spokane Reservation,
Three Mile Island—

radioactive forever.
The feminization of everything
is required.

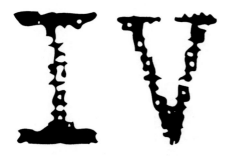

IV

Journey to the Root

Janine Canan

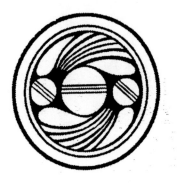

*Blood must flow
for the garden to flower.
And the heart that loves
is a wound without shield.*

—Rumi

1 THE LOVER

Meeting My Fate

My white dog pulled me to the door. I knocked, and it opened. A magnificent woman rose off her chair, greeting me in a voice that pealed like an old mission bell. I shrank back, and pulled my dog with me. I hadn't even bothered to change my clothes—still had on jeans and a white tee shirt painted with pink and turquoise symbols. It was a hot afternoon.

Along the wall I slunk toward a table where our hostess had set out the drinks. Pouring myself a tall tonic, I glanced around the room. The only empty seat was a small chair nestled against the body of the large woman, who I now saw wore black.

I sipped my drink slowly, thinking. There was no other place to sit. Resolutely, I stepped toward the uncomfortable stool, and squatted down. I leaned as far forward as possible, keeping my eyes lowered to the carpet—so I couldn't see her.

But she had already resumed her commanding tone. I can stop this, I imagined—ejaculating syllables sharp and cold as ice cubes. However, as the last sound melted in air, something snared my attention. I lifted my head lightly. On her broad breast sleeping birds lay suspended—turquoise, white and shining onyx.

How beautiful! I gasped with uncontrollable passion. I raised my face all the way up to her luminous smile. Her eyes were beaming. One was an exquisite sapphire that reflected the wide blue sky. The other contained a broken iris that sprawled into darkness.

The Lover

Your skin was midnight satin.
And I was a brilliant seeker.

Your heart was mother of pearl.
And I was a baby oyster.

Your voice was doting honey.
And I was parched for sweetness.

Your eyes divined other worlds.
And I was a starry stranger.

Your mind was a windblown encyclopedia.
And I was a frantic scholar.

Your words were silken knots.
And I was a master of paradox.

Your lotus opened a thousand petals.
And I was a bee—I dove to your center.

The Joy

Along the hills of your body
I rooted in the fragrant earth.

Stretching my blossoming arms,
I heaved with offerings.

I was a peach dripping gold,
and you drank me.

I was a comet that tumbled
across your moonlit valley.

I was a cry in the forest,
that pierced your windy heart.

I was a woolly lamb in your pen,
who was stripped by the shearing night.

Listen! In the bleeding womb of life
there are rhythms that can never be broken....

Erotic

by Marguerite Yourcenar (translation)

You the hornet, and I the rose.
You the spume, and I the rock.
In this strange metamorphosis
you the phoenix, and I the pyre.

You Narcissus, and I the spring,
my eyes reflecting your emotion.
You the treasure, and I the coffer.
I the tide—the swimmer inside me.

And you—mouth upon mouth—
the languor lulling the fever,
the billow dissolving in the waves.

But whatever this tender game,
the soul on fire always flying away—
exquisite gold bird—in the wide blue sky.

Fourteenth Elegy

by Frances Jammes (translation)

My Love, you said. *My Love,* I answered.
It's snowing, you said. *Snowing,* I answered.

Still, you said. *Still,* I answered.
So it is, you said. *So it is,* I answered you.

Later on you told me, *I love you.* And I replied,—*More than ever.*
The lovely summer is ending, you said. —*It's autumn,*

I replied. And our words were no longer the same.
Finally one day you said, *Oh Beloved, I love you so much.*

(just as vast Autumn gloriously descended).
And I responded, *Tell me again—*

Mourning Doves

What is that sound? I asked.
Mourning doves, you answered, *nesting in the eaves.*
The fir brushed against the window in warning.
Azaleas rushed every red into bloom.
Then suddenly Spring had to end—
their thick throaty voices were calling.
You were the first to wake—from the bedroom you went.
Your voice too became thick—with impatience,
stoic deception, brilliant betrayals.

I woke with an anguished start.
No! was all I could say—I was shouting.
In my tone the frenzied flames were mounting.
I ran to your rolling hills, that always consoled me,
but there lay an empty valley.
Oh, why did you leave me to follow the mourning doves
that nested while we were sleeping?
Their voices were lush with seduction—
like yours, Beloved, before you flew away.

2 FOOL'S GOLD

A Cat Climbs

A cat climbs onto the downy bed
and steps toward the magnificent woman
who stretches out her hand.
Tilting her rosy palm like a cup,
she pours herself into the tiny furry body
that arches hungrily to drink.

Soon the cat is humming like a cello.
But already the woman is tired
of the fragile electric yearning
that floods the room with thrilling music.
With one grand sweep of her hand
she empties the dregs—and sends the cat flying.

Detour

I
Here, you forgot something.
—It's your love.

I found it after you left.

II
You fell upon me in the night,
dripping honey—
were you Beauty
or her brother Cruelty?

I fought you for a fat fist of tears.

III
Sack of lonely,
so full of tears, *whys* and fierce farewells;
yet empty
whenever my heart cried,

Hold me.

IV
See you on the solstice,
when the light is gone.
See you in another's eyes,
when love has died.
See you in a dream,
when I sleep alone at night.

See you 'round....

Rubies

Rubies, it's not your fault
you were given in passion.

Rubies, it's not your fault
you were pried from your bed.

Rubies, it's not your fault
you were crystallized with lies.

Rubies, it's not your fault
you were bloodied by love.

Rubies, it's not your fault....

The Last Supper

The Gods have prepared the last supper.
Dali winks and sets down the appetizer,
twirling his moustache.
Mermaid sauté, poppies fumés,
and *aperitif* of tears, *spécialité de la maison*.
A whirling dakini dishes up the entrée:
bloody buffalo in scorpion sauce
served in a basket of woven women.

Followed by a bowl of moonstone-glazed
ochre sand—decorated
with a diamond cross
and garnished with two gold rings.
Offered with sour lemons and bitter bread.
For dessert, the couple enjoy frozen hope
with burnt cream, and a final toast
of finest champagne—from the widow's private cellar.

After supper, the lovers arise
and step onto a path dimly lit with skulls.
Marigolds, furry magenta petals
and a million dead birds strew the way.
Past holy black Bastet,
and inextinguishable shining Artemis
with her mighty bow and yelping hounds—
their way leads down forever.

Miss Maya

Miss Maya, how do you do
in your fine pointy shoes?

Miss Maya, from your charm
came nothing but harm.

Miss Maya, it was dazzling
and maddening, but now that I see—

Miss Maya, dearest, farewell.

Janine Canan

Important

On a spring Sunday evening we met.
You announced your name
as if it were important.
And I wondered, why you thought so.

You seduced me with your smile,
a sun that wept warmth.
And the stone birds flew
over your abundant breast.

I wanted to hold your hand.
But it was already time for you to go.
So long, Important One,
with a dazzling eye and—oh—a cruel one.

Once Upon a Bedroom

The empty bedroom
is where the fir came through the window,
stroking our cheeks.

The empty bedroom is where
I saw you, and you saw me
in love's jeweled mirror.

The empty bedroom
is where we romped and stomped
our toppling shrine to once-upon-a-time.

Fool's Gold

Goddess, would I do it all over again?

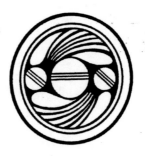

3 LAMENTATIONS

Sarangi Sorrow

Against the carnelian sky
a young man sits on the palace pool steps
and plays the Sarangi his father once played.
Bow to string, he plays his soul.

Together we wander the white-walled labyrinth,
kneel upon dirt, drink sweet mint—
he can tell by the way I listen
some violent music has shattered my heart.

Oh, nothing sobs like the Sarangi—
it whines in the empty cavity,
it saws through grief till you worship grief
releasing its sundering song.

The young man's eyes are bright springs.
Each note climbs out of mud dripping gold.
For nothing surpasses the grandeur of Sarangi sorrow—
sixteen thousand miles I voyaged to hear this sound,

that drowns discarded love in raptured joy.
Oh, nothing is sweeter than humiliation Sarangi plays—
like jasmine it rises from tinkling dust.
Beneath the towers in deepening desert dusk

a young man plays like his grandfathers;
for queens and strangers he plays
till night has drunk every tone. *Where are you—*
Sarangi cries—*among all these milky moping golden stars.*

Abandoned Garden

In front we planted purple periwinkle stars.
Under lacy heavenly bamboo
they sprawled around two towering pines.
Over the fence gushed escallonia's rosy blooms.

Then the hillside steeply declined—
along the steps cheery marguerites,
shy coral bells you planted on your knees,
then ruffled, puffed-up, proud red rhodies.

In the corner anemones floated their clouds of silk;
in the flower box, fluorescent pink and fiery red,
madly muttering impatiens
I watered with my tears.

By the pale blue door azaleas bled
onto the silent horrified rose.
Near the hostile mailbox the maiden dogwood
never dared bloom her tender pink.

The infected maple struggled to spread her roots.
On the meadow wildflowers multiplied
in a thick green carpet where we might have lain,
tucked in each other's blossoming hearts.

Crazy Raccoon

It's the crazy raccoon, says the boy next door,
screaming every night when it turns dark,
at the highest pitch, inconsolably.

Am I that crazy raccoon?
For my heart still turns itself inside-out
for you, who long ago left without a glance.

Like a razor the raccoon's cry cuts the night.
But no scream stirs your caring back to life.
My love grows lush and thorny

like blackberries over a vast dead tree.
The raccoon falls silent—night rings in my ears
as I lie on the soft peach quilts we once slept in.

Only my head on your breast told what was in my heart.
Had I known you set the alarm so early,
I would have stayed up all night

pouring syrup to the bottom of your soul.
I would have knelt, adoring every second of night.
Ah, didn't I try? You slept—I couldn't wake you!

Not even the shrieking raccoon pierces your locked heart.
If only I had left out every word that wasn't love,
it mourns inconsolably, whenever it turns dark.

Your Name

by Marguerite Yourcenar (translation)

Your name, given to you by your mother.
Your name, poured down my bitter throat like a drop of poisoned honey.
Your name, that I cried under every sky and wept in every bed.
Your name, that I read in the water-marks on every page of my misery.
Your name, clear as the tear shed on us by one of the Angels.
Your name, like a beautiful naked child who rolled in the mud.
Your name, that bruises my mouth.
Your name, with which I sleep like a talisman.
Your name, like a sentence which condemns me to banishment.
Your name, that I moan like a beggar who continues her lament
even at the gates of a city gone up in flames.
Your name, where so many sordid stories perch like flies.
Your name, that people speak as if it were just anyone's.
Your name, X for the unknown that is your self.
Your baptismal name, inscribed in the black register of the Devil
and the golden book of God.
Your name, that nothing could ever make me forget.
Your name, with your memory the only thing you can never take
from me, since anyone under blue heaven may utter it.
Your name, each letter of which is a nail in my crucifixion.
Your name, the only one I'll remember on Resurrection morning.

Heartbreak

How could you, stone by stone, tear down our house,
where rooms flared from the spiraling center
and doves cooed in the dreaming sun.

How could you contemptuously turn
and rage down our aspiring tower,
that gazed beyond bridges into every direction.

How could you abandon those spaces young and yearning,
gutting our cupboard, bed and hearth,
while the sun gilded the West with sacred fire.

How could you storm past hummingbirds sipping
at fuchsia altars, and flee the guardian pines at the gate,
just as I shattered, and our love was born.

Betrayal in the Lotus

The door is closed.
The house snuggles into the hillside,
newly planted with rapid orange impatiens.

The whole hill rests in the slope of an open heart,
whose vibrant petals once rose and fell
in loving prayer.

One by one the tender petals were shredded
and torn from their dutiful stem;
yet the battered stem

miraculously bloomed again—
vaster, more dazzling, in every petal
a world of jeweled light.

Still, deep in the shade of one purple petal
stands that house brightly lit, where unfaithful
lovers lie—deliriously content.

In Your Mailbox

In your mailbox I placed a yellow dandelion
that climbed through the grass—

it was already limp as I laid it
upon the pile of unopened mail.

When you (or was it your new lover)
removed the mail from the box,

did you find, effacing itself among
the sealed envelopes, a lifeless strand.

Did your heart pause remembering
the vibrant golden cloth from which it came.

Wedding Bells

Long ago I planted this love,
that rose into a towering tree.
It was you who raised the axe,
that chopped it down.

Now stubborn shoots
offer their sorrow
up to the searing light.
Our roots go deeper than existence.

In you I built
my heart's golden temple.
When you tore it out—
was it God or I who cried?

At last dying ends.
Triumphant, death arrives.
In grief's sunken cathedral,
our wedding bells chime:

Though you love a thousand others,
you will always be mine.

The Exile

I always wanted to love your wild flowering fields,
climb your narrowest passes,
rise through snow to the gathering clouds,
and pierce like rain your wet black soil.

I always wanted to breathe with the seeds,
spread my broad green leaves,
sprout buds bursting with heady fragrances
and shed sumptuous petals at your feet.

I always wanted to release every golden fruit,
sleep through the slow groaning ice
and waken on your jubilant meadow—
but I was exiled to this world of immortal complaint.

The Weeping Tree

I am the weeping tree,
that weeps and weeps.

I am the weeping tree,
that seeps and seeps.

I am the weeping tree,
that steeps and steeps.

I am the weeping tree,
that keeps and keeps.

I am the weeping tree,
that weeps and weeps.

My Grief

Queen, my broken
tall grass—
I never knew
that you were mine.

Prayer to Love Sorrow

by Francis Jammes (translation)

I have only my sorrow, and want nothing more.
She has been and still is faithful.
What more could I wish, since in those hours
when my soul was crushed beneath my heart,
she was there, seated at my side.
Oh Sorrow, you see, finally I have come to respect you,
for I know you will never depart.
Ah, I admit you were forced to become beautiful—
you who never left the pitiful hearth
of my poor black heart.
Oh my Sorrow, you are better than a beloved.
For I know, on the day of my death you will be here,
still—oh Sorrow—trying to invade my heart.

Offering My Tears

Here are my tears, tall pitchers of tears.
I pour them round you,
so you may grow more and more beautiful.

As the cedar offers its sheltering arms,
as the house offers its shield from piercing winds,
as the sky offers its lumined breath,
as the crow offers its urgent call—
so I offer these salty tears,
wept from the fathomless ocean of love.

Pitchers and pitchers of shining tears—
as I pour them
may I grow more and more aware.

4 THE GODDESSES

Starlings

I let go, but this love
won't leave me—
it circles and returns
like a flock of starlings.

Which way does the sky go?
And how will I get over
the barrier of your body,
rolling green to the boundless horizon.

Oh, how the starlings in majestic formation
soar—euphoric over rising
mounds, where layer on layer
civilizations lie down in star-dust.

But starlings never forget—
like a deck of magic cards shuffling
they fall and reunite,
scattering the tall calm sky with their glitter.

Janine Canan

The Meditation

I meditated upon you deeply
and we became one.
Now, no matter how far away,
you live in my heart.

My heart is a satin coffin
I tend with pungent flowers and prayers.
My heart is a hand-carved cradle
I rock and rock.

I meditated upon you deeply
and we became one.
Now, no matter how long ago,
you live in my heart.

The Treasure Box

Your nightmares will always be safe
in my treasure box—painted
with crimson blossoms, enchanting birds.

Your nightmares belong with your jewels—
carnelian dreams, melting amber,
lazuli skies teeming with golden stars.

There, whenever a child cries—
rivers rush turquoise, hearts pour ruby,
mirrors reflect only the night's beauty.

Karmic Forest

It wasn't our fault—the Gods sundered us.
We were two tall trees growing together,
bark in bark, our inner rings locked.

Was it Kali wielded the axe, that seared
our bodies crimson, sliced our tightly woven roots—
riding out of Durga's forehead, her tongue beheading the world?

We teetered, swayed and must have fainted,
crashing into the silence—now our torn roots
that reveled in thirst, are stone coils seeking nothing.

So let the little children climb up
on our throne-like trunks, that will lie rotting
in the glistening wet for centuries to come.

And our scaly green fronds, that drank the light
and filled the forest with breath—
let the crows pluck these rusty wands for their nests.

No, it wasn't our fault—fate demanded this death.
Every scene was perfectly staged—and we,
let it forever be said, were magnificent falling.

Whenever New Hearts Break

by Heinrich Heine (translation)

Whenever new hearts break,
the stars above burst into laughter.
Laughing, they call down the blue distance:

Poor human beings
love with all their souls,
yet torment and torture each other to death.

We have never known this love
so fatal to the poor beings below—
that is why we are immortal.

My Handle

This axe in my heart
is a stunning object
splitting my days.
Frozen long ago,
it forms a strong handle
for the Goddess to pick me up.

Mysteries in the Garden

The little fat girl sits and swings
and swings. From the house
voices rise strident and cruel.
Clouds glister on the water—everything shivers.
Higher and higher, she swings in silence.

*

An old man chops down two rose trees,
inextricably twined over an arbor.
Stacks logs by the stump of the fire rose—
to burn or plant anew.
The woman waits for a cutting of the deeper red.

*

Scratching at the dirt, her fingers burning,
she digs up the bones, and cries hoarsely
Give me what I need!
We can't, they mutter, dissolving in the dust,
disappointing her for the last time.

*

Two lilies float—for a moment no suffering,
only stillness of the violet water.
Hope disappears in the gauzy white petals.
Light enters the yellow stamen.
Powdery pads float on the surface.

*

In one hand the Goddess holds the scythe—
in the other She holds the golden seed.
At Her feet a woman kneels.
Flames flare up, and slowly curl
their charcoal petals over the past.

*

A woman buried herself in the garden.
Now out of a poppy field—roaring red,
tender pink, burnished green, she rises.
Mauve and blue trees enter her
as she spreads in the wide gold dusk.

May I Forget

May I forget you, my Love,
in the silver sun that flares in the wintering sky,
in the misty mountain, poised on the horizon,
that ponders the motionless lake.

Along this quiet winding tar-dark road
where the gull above the mauve and leafless branch
flails her casual arm, crossing to a world beyond—
oh Love, may I forget.

The Goddesses

Every being is immortal, says the first Goddess.
May demons not crouch on your chest, says the second.
Eyes of the third Goddess well with tenderness.
The fourth radiates young life.
Very very hard, utters the fifth.
More work to be done—says the sixth—*first sit in the sun.*
The seventh delights, *Is your heart broken?*
The eighth bursts with righteous indignation.
The ninth will not judge.
Tenth Goddess cries, *I'm coming!*
The eleventh sighs, *There is nothing to be done.*
Beyond this pain, coos the twelfth, *are treasures.*
Everything, proclaims the thirteenth Goddess,
is perfect as it is.

In the City of Death

Vacationing in the city of Death,
where people come to be burned to ash
and swept back to the holy river;

asleep in my hotel bed surrounded
by thousands of pointing temples
dedicated to Lord Death—

I dreamed you died.
And started to steer my course back
to find out if you had left any word—for me.

There was no reason to believe you had—
long ago I heard your heart click shut.
Then silence noisily devoured you.

When you drop your cryptic body,
Naked Spirit, where will you go—
will you ever return with some final word?

Janine Canan

The Slow River that Winds

Should we meet again after many lives,
it will be as if only an instant has passed—
a tiny glitch in time's machinery,
a slip in the memory of the soul.

Certainly I will know the turn of your shoulder,
the spark quickening in your eye—
for I love you like my own life
and I will always love you.

The Elements of Love

The house is locked,
but I am the earth
and truer than fear.

The house is cold,
but I am the air
and truer than remorse.

The house is burning,
but I am the water
and truer than fury.

The house is gone,
but I am the fire
and truer than grief.

A Glass of Ruby

Pour me another glass of ruby—
I'm used to your fire now.

Whenever you smile,
demons frolic with angels.

When I drink the wine you hand me,
I am razed again to the ground.

I'm used to being earth now—
all the precious jewels grow within.

And so I begin to love myself as I am—
pour me another glass of ruby!

Wild Music

You are playing your music again,
and I run after each golden tone.

Suddenly I ring like a gong struck by God.
Oh, my heart is indestructible
whenever you play on it.

Strike me, Beloved, again and again.
Never stop sounding my wild thunder heart.

5 AND I RELEASE YOU

Two Pears

We were two pears hanging on a tree.
You were gold, and I—still green.
I thought we would always be together.
One day a violent wind took you instantly.

You plunged to the loamy world below.
While I, left hanging—growing juicier,
was soon devoured by a throng of raucous birds,
whose bittersweet song now you hear.

Can Love Die

Can love die—like an azalea
that once was covered with cherry-red lips
and now is nothing but bald pricks,
a tangled ball of in-grown roots.

Doesn't something cling still—a fine knot
of denial, a last ember of betrayal,
some inaudibly gnawing guilt
or anguished gaping loss.

Or does even grief die—so that painlessly
I can pull you out of my rocky soil
and watch you blow away like a weed
that dashes after the escaping horizon.

At memory's cool reunion, your soft skin
wears the untouchable shroud.
Yet the azaleas keep blooming—
shocking magenta, cremating crimson, immortal gold....

Divine Abandoner

Goodbye, happiness
we never knew, and flames we threw.

Goodbye, tender fiend,
precious connoisseur, and final editor.

Goodbye, oh silly idea
of saying *goodbye.*

Until we crumble and form more true—
Goodbye, Goodbye....

Rainbow

Rainbow, in her burning orange arms,
held my heart, that broke and healed.

Rainbow, arching blue,
held the thin bridge over the mirroring bay.

Rainbow, blushing red,
held love long gone and far away.

Rainbow, in her broad violet hat,
held the clouds, both dark and light.

Rainbow, striding forth in her golden shoes,
held the hills, turning green again.

Janine Canan

The Answer

Where is the hill
that rested my head?

Where is the air
that breathed in my song?

Where is the stream
that succored my wound?

Where is the fire
that took my heart?

Nest Always in Love

Nest always in love, my Love,
where every twiggy death
tufts softly round.

Nest in this worn basket
with all the jewels—
midnight's lightening bloods.

Nest in this heart, large
enough to hold more than joy—
larger even than grief.

Nest in this prayer, shed
in the ever-decaying world—
to be born in a love vaster yet.

Janine Canan

Mirabeau Bridge

by Guillaume Apollinaire (translation)

Under Mirabeau Bridge flows the Seine—
and our loves.
Must I be reminded.
Joy always follows the pain.

Though night comes, the hour strikes.
The days disappear—I remain.

Let us stand face to face
and hand in hand,
while that weary wave of Eternal Glances
passes under the bridge of our arms.

Though night comes, the hour strikes,
the days disappear—I remain.

Love disappears like this flowing water—
love disappears.
How slow is life,
and hope—how violent.

Though night comes, the hour strikes,
the days disappear—I remain.

Days pass, and weeks pass.
Neither time past
nor our loves come again.
Under Mirabeau Bridge flows the Seine.

Though night comes, the hour strikes,
the days disappear—I remain.

Love

by Mirabai (translation)

Do not mention the word *love*,
my naive companion.
The path turns strange,
once you offer your love.
Your body is crushed at the first step.
If you want to offer love,
be prepared to cut off your head
and sit on it.
Circle the lamp like a moth
and shed your body.
Present your head like a deer
who hears the hunter's horn.
Swallow burning coals like a partridge
in love with the moon.
Yield your life like a fish
parted from the ocean.
Surrender like a bee
caught in closing lotus petals.

Mira's Beloved lifted a mountain
with one little finger.
She says, Offer your mind to Those lotus feet.

The Ceremony

This is the town, where good and evil live.
This is the lover, who does not forget.
This is the beloved, who could not catch the golden ring.
This is the Goddess, whose shining body is the world.
This is the candle, that lights the moment.
This is the bell, that rings release.

And I Release You

And I release you
to fly away.
And I release you
to love another.
And I release you
to forget.

And I release the infant fingers
of my clinging heart.
And I release the perfect petals
of my open heart.
And I release the ancient ache
of my empty heart.

And I stand before you naked,
soul to soul.
And I release my love
to the One it came from.
And I bathe in the towering tumbling
fountain of light.

And I surrender.

Epilogue

I thought you were my Love,
but you were only a lesson.

I thought you were my home,
but you were only a station.

I thought you were my song,
but you were only a rehearsal.

I thought you were my Goddess,
but you were only human.

Vale of Kashmir

The love I thought was gold
was tinsel and dross.

The smile I thought the sun
set in a storm of shattering.

Today I drive past those stuttering flames.
Love is the only lover I want.

Changing Woman

(A Navajo Story Told Again)

Beauty before you,
Beauty behind you,
Beauty above you,
Beauty below you.

—Navajo Chant

Changing Woman

Long long ago Dawn came to Darkness, and Changing Woman was orn. Golden rays of light carried her from the sky to a mountain top. The our Winds swept down and breathed life into her, printing spirals on her ingers, head and toes. The Flowers surrounded and cradled her. Joyfully, the lue Birds sang.

The Holy People, who lived below, sent Talking God up the mountain o find out what all the commotion was about. When Talking God reached he top, he found a beautiful baby girl lying in the grass. Gathering her into is arms, he carried her down the mountain. The People were delighted by er, and fed her pollen, animal broth and dew from the loveliest flowers. The ittle girl ran races. And Talking God sang to her. In four days, she was fully rown.

Bright red rain fell from inside her. The People stroked and painted her, ressing her in the finest deer-skin, shells and turquoise. *She moves,* they sang. *he moves, she moves, she moves.* While they sang, she changed into an old voman. Then she changed back into a young woman. Again she changed nto an old woman. And again she changed back into a young woman. Old, oung, old, young—four times she changed, until she had become the finest oung woman.

One day, when Changing Woman was out gathering seeds and berries, un came riding by on his white horse, wearing his whitest clothes. Stunned y the young woman's beauty, he blazed brilliantly, begging her to follow him n his journey to the far West. But Changing Woman protested. *I would be oo lonely,* She replied. Still Sun persisted, *Follow me, and we will be closer than e have ever been.*

Finally Changing Woman was persuaded. And stepping on the back of a og, she followed Sun westward to a majestic wild mountain, located in the iddle of the ocean. Wind and Light came along to help Changing Woman uild her new house. In the East, where Sun stood in the morning, they built room entirely of white shell. In the West, they made a room of yellow balone. Black Thunder arrived from the North, and sat down by a black corn-alk—there they built a room of pure black jet. In the South, they made a rquoise room with a turquoise door, and turquoise footprints leading to it.

Changing Woman's house was constructed of four stories, with ladder leading to each one. Little suns were placed in every room. In the center of the house, they built a rock crystal altar reflecting every color in the rainbow. There, in Crystal House, Changing Woman lived happily with Sun. She spat hailstones to clear the land of monsters. And one day, while resting below shimmering waterfall, she conceived the twins, Monster Slayer and Child of the Waters.

Changing Woman taught the twins all her songs and dances. When they were fully grown, she put prayer sticks in their blankets and sent them on their way. Then she let out a piercing cry, that wrapped the whole island in grief. She rubbed skin off her body, and stirring into it shells, stone, sand clay, pollen and foam—she made Chickens, Dogs, Goats, Sheep, Antelope and Horses. Finally, so she would never be lonely, she created Human Beings. She gave them pets, and stone canes for drawing water from the desert. Lifting her great bow, she shot rainbows into them—then blew them out over the wide ocean.

When Changing Woman was very old, so old she could barely move, Talking God reappeared at her door. This time he brought with him Human boy and girl. In a flash, they had traveled on a bright rainbow to the coast, then crossed the green ocean on an underwater spiral. They followed the white trail to her house, and greeted the Four Directions. When Changing Woman's door opened, they saw the most beautiful young woman they had ever seen, dancing joyfully before her crystal altar. The children bowed. Changing Woman bathed them in her crystal bowl, dressed them in white and put feathers in their hair.

She sang:

> *Beauty before you,*
> *Beauty behind you,*
> *Beauty above you,*
> *Beauty below you.*
> *Walk now with Beauty around you*
> *and your way will be beautiful.*

Then Changing Woman sat down under a cornstalk. Blue Bird sat on corn tassel. And Changing Woman sang every song she knew. Dancing through the pollen, she left her golden footprints everywhere.

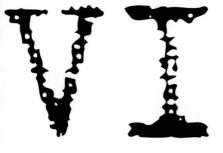

VI

In The Mother's Heart

O Mother, everything is You.
You Yourself are everything.
There is nothing but You, O Mother.

—Karunalaye Devi Chant

Janine Canan

1 DAWN

My Heart

My heart is pouring itself out of me.
My heart is soaring toward you over thousands of miles.
My heart comes nearer and nearer.
My heart longs to enter...

Like ten fingers running over the keys,
like a powerful stream that has ever been flowing,
like a flock of night birds lit by the moon—
I am flying after my heart.....

Scars Publications and Design 115

Reflect

Reflect on the dark
where fear is lost.

Reflect on the dark
where light begins.

Reflect on the dark
where gold is dancing.

A Dream

The old white house is painted green—
bougainvillea once climbed to the roof,
avocado sheltered my sleep.
Who lives there now? No one I know.
Who lived there—a dream.

Around the block I ran
to a low brick wall where I sat
drying my tears in pale moonbeams.
Who lives there now? No one I know.
Who lived there—a dream.

The old house stares in a smog basin—
peach trees gone, rose beds empty
where I made mud pies with honey.
Who lives there now? No one I know.
Who lived there—a dream.

Expect Nothing

Expect nothing. What you are looking for you will never find in huma
beings. Even what you expect in yourself will change tomorrow. You wi
change your mind, or your mind will change you. There is something you ca
expect, but what is it? You cannot expect anything of nature—unpredictabl
magnificent, dangerous, ever-changing. What about the Gods' stormy dr
mas? Expect everything, yet expect nothing. Kali—Creator, Sustaine
Destroyer—is the God for you.

Expect nothing. Memorize this: *Expect nothing.* Even death is unce
tain—they say we live on. Expect meanings far beyond your ken, or capaci
to comprehend. Expect to suffer, expect to desire. Expect rare moments
relief. Expect love to disappoint you. Expect to fail. Expect cruelty, harr
guilt, misery and remorse. Do not expect tenderness—it will surprise you. D
not expect beauty—its omnipresence will sate you to numbness and disple
sure.

Expect nothing. Then you will be ready for the forms to fly away, leavi
the only thing you can expect, that is always here. Expect Nothing. Acce
Nothing. Embrace Nothing. It is good, this Nothing that is everywhere—
full of disappointment, dissolution, release. It will come any moment now-

Not Having a Child

What is it like not to have a child?
It is like going on an ocean voyage in a canoe
without compass or map.

It is like standing on the desert under a wide open sky.
Your body grieves, your body cries—
no one to recognize you as their own, as home.

Alone in conversation with your being,
you must turn your back on death,
and talk directly to All That Is.

Evening Grace

To Marianne

The cat perches on the window sill
over banks of bright peach fog.
Piano melodies lilt on the radio.
A dog howls plaintively.
The cards show a death—midstream
the scorpion bit the camel it rode, and drowned.

In the violet light I take the chalice
and let the Graces dance.
A light breeze lifts my hair
and strokes my face, dissolving the cruelty
inflicted by thinking I was the author of fate.
The cat contemplates the orange and blue evening.

Earth Talks

Beneath the spongy wet grass
the stream talks to me.
Conversations among the trees
swirl through my hair.
The full moon whispers
behind my back.

In its tight cage my own heart whines.
My white dog lies beside me, panting.
All night Earth babbles
her incessant pulsing stream.
And the frightened disappear.
There is no one but us—

Pieces

Oh, the commotion
of the ocean, the commotion
of the ocean.....

*

I was cautiously
tapping my way
toward God.....

*

If every day is an eternity,
any sentence
is easily a bomb.....

*

Always more of this dross
rattling around
in the bottom of heaven.....

*

This gaze at this weeping
that waters earth
into bloom, is God.

Janine Canan

O Mind, Worship
by Mirabai (translation)

O Mind, worship the lotus feet
that cannot be destroyed.
Between heaven and earth everything passes away.
Why fast or make pilgrimages?
Why bother with abstract talk?
Why attempt suicide under the blades of Benares?
Life is but the play of sparrows—
it ends with the onset of night.
Why don an ochre robe, and go wandering?
Whatever you wear, if you do not enter the Source,
you will be caught in the net of return.

Mira loves Krishna.
She cries, *Sever every knot in my heart!*

Oh Kali

Hi Kali, come on in.
I've been waiting for You
in this loneliness
that prefers even the company of Death
to nothing—
to You alone
I bow down.

*

Kali, only You are great enough
to take this deafening confusion
overflowing with pain
and topped with resistance—
a dish appropriate
only for You,
Glorious Tongue.

*

Oh Kali, vast and voluptuous
are your flames—engulfing,
devouring, triumphant.
Only You can swallow this seething,
becoming more beautiful,
graceful and tender—
Divine Daughter, All Powerful!

*

You who bring grief,
You who destroy beauty,
You who abandon lovers,
You who betray human hope—
stronger and more violent than Death,
You force me open, Great One.
My heart is too small—I'm shattering—

The Stars

by Simone Weil (translation)

Stars on fire, that populate the night's far sky,
mute stars, revolving blind, forever glazed—
you yank yesterdays out of our hearts,
and throw us on tomorrows without our consent.
And we cry to you, but all our cries are in vain.

We follow you since we must—arms linked,
eyes lifted to your pure, but bitter light.
From your viewpoint all our suffering means little.
And so silent, we stagger on—until suddenly
your divine fire is here—in our hearts.

Janine Canan

Knowledge

A spike through reality—
blazing red ember
in snowheart.

Cliff's Edge

As I walk the cliff's edge,
the sun throws open her cape
and the ocean flashes a million mirrors.
Suddenly the dark one
shoves a gleaming blade to my heart.
The sun bursts into blazing stars.

Dropping my name,
I fall down before my pain—
What shall I do? I cry.
Accept everything that I give you,
She answers. *I am everything—*
you are burning with My Life.

Mira and Krishna

Mira sleeps in her grandfather's palace,
and dreams of marrying Krishna.
Krishna grazes his cows by the flowing river.

Mira dances before his image waving ghee-lights.
Krishna poises on the back
of a gold and black-spotted snake.

Mira eats the meal in-laws serve
with a cup of poison.
Krishna folds his legs in a lotus blossom.

Mira unbraids her hair, marks herself with fiery color.
Krishna gazes under petalled brows,
dark curls on blue shoulders.

Mira takes the temple road,
the palace gates slam shut behind her.
Krishna snaps off a reed, heaves a sigh of relief.

Mira sings, laughing and clapping.
Krishna jumps off the serpent's back
into the deepest waters.

Mira grabs his foot
and spirals into the current.
Krishna's crocodile earring snags her swollen heart.

Mira is a pyre of aloe and sandalwood.
Krishna heats his long cool limbs
in her fragrant flames.

Mira sways in the crowd,
the universe swirling round her ankles.
Krishna sits in motionless contemplation.

Mira's heart is a wide open lily.
Krishna is the dusky breeze
that slashes her petals.

Mira tramps across country, begging and seeking.
Krishna plays his bamboo flute
seated on her head.

Mira thirsts for every drop,
yet suffocates in the aroma.
Krishna is beauty, the dazzling musician.

Mira wraps herself in a crimson sari,
lights incense, and opens her bed.
Krishna winks and vanishes.

Mira gnaws on love, her eyes unclosing.
Krishna is a thorny bush
in the night never ending.

Mira grows proud and angry,
her senses greedy.
Krishna is the bottomless well of rage and grief.

Mira boils with fear, shame, doubt and disgust.
Krishna powders himself
with her soft ashes.

Mira beholds the circular saws
used for beheading.
Krishna's crown is radiant with diamonds and rubies.

Mira hears thunder, pounds her big drum.
Krishna, where are you, the peacock cries,

the lotus lounges in moonlight.

Mira rows through her tears,
her heart grows fat as a mango.
Krishna pours himself into the octopus ocean.

Mira carries a golden pitcher on her head.
Krishna overflows
and floods the earth with green.

Mira hears his footstep
that crushes her heart with joy.
Krishna swings a rosary of perfect tears.

Mira unbolts the door, her white hair flowing.
Krishna's eyes are dark coppery clouds
with lightning.

Mira drenched in love
cries, *Darling!*
Krishna returns the love everlasting.

Mira takes his hand, and rises out of her body.
Krishna plays a rapturous melody
upon it.

Mira's song emanates
to the farthest corner.
Krishna dances blissfully on the rim of the dark.

*N*aive

I was naive—when the rainbow
landed at my feet, I stuck my hand
into its molten pot of gold.

And so I, too, turned to gold—all my past
melted like fuming plastic, and I grieved
for every taste that wasn't the honey of union.

Now nothing but gentleness can hold me.
I was naive—but now, when that arc of blazing color
opens at my feet, I bow to its bowl of transforming gold.

2 ONE BEING

The Stones

Along the beach stones,
exposed by the retreating tide,
greet me like friends from long ago.

And I bend to gather
eggs, mounds, ovals, crescents
smoothed by life in the tumbling sea.

Some broken by a catastrophic blow
reveal inside a glittering gold.
As I walk the studded shore

they pound in my loving hand—
heartbeats of the crumbling earth
I shall one day let go.

Saved in the Snow

The cedars approach
in long white gowns,
and a wide white veil
blows across my windshield.

Suddenly my car skates on ice
and I am diaphanous prayer.
Arms stretch—in waves
I rise toward the moon.

The car spins into a snowy ditch
like a babe to its cradle.
Here is your body, a voice calls.
And I look at my new white hands—amazed.

Janine Canan

Madrona Mother

At the cliff's edge
I sit upon Your deepening root,
Your foliage vast
above my wondering head.

And the Moon comes sowing diamonds
down the darkened strait,
and kneels beneath
Your mighty feet.

Again and again, You lean out
over the crumbling abyss,
and gather us back
in Your molting red limbs.

Forest Temple

The forests are falling—
they roll down the hills like tears.
And beyond these cemeteries
the last firs draw back, shuddering.

Then deeper I must go to find
that temple where the kinglets chime,
guarded by an elk priest whose beard
flows along fern carpet.

In greeny gold of the first cathedral
Earth grows long and slow.
Through mossy arches blackbirds glide
past thousand-year-old spruces.

High upon a hemlock
the red-crested woodpecker drums.
Kneeling inside Her fragrant heart,
I exhale Her radiant light.

One Being

To Carol Fabric

Out of the live oak forest
a doe steps onto the thick green lawn,
stomping her foot.

My old wolf-dog lowers her nose
on the wood porch, watching.
Wide-eyed and -eared the doe approaches.

Crow caws at every step.
Squirrel races down a slender branch;
Mosquito circles, buzzing.

The whole hill rattles with crickets.
And cars below roar like the ocean
as she gazes into me, and I into her—at One Being.

Two Eagles

To Susan Scott

Below the mountain white and solitary
we stretch out on the emerald hill,
emptying our bottle of flowery champagne.

Walking the watery shore we spot
on the upper branch of a fir high on the cliff
two eagles big as humans.

She's shy, you say as yards of black wing
spread across the sky. And he turns his large
gold-beaked head to watch her fly.

Waves

As I walk the wet sand
watching for Northern lights,
sun already gone,
my white dog a searchlight,
waves clapping in the wind,
all the teary voices rush into my ears
and my hair whips in the night.

Everything they tell me.
I go deeper in the suffering
and am flooded with the meaning,
foam feet running toward mine.
The lights come on—
of the city we are building.
My white dog waves her friendly tail
and stars appear.

Cold invades my heart with love.
Alive, they say, *alive.*
My white dog sits, and she hears too.
We are all waves—
roaring and whispering,
daring and retreating
and once more daring to love.

Janine Canan

Snowfall

Fat little junco
in black silk hood
stuffs from thistle feeder
dangling under snow-filled eaves.

While flakes
flutter from feather heaven,
ski the edge of wind,
thud off bushy cedar's burdened limbs.

Behind my window I step
too close, and away he flies.
When I yield my pen to glories of white—
he returns to feast under the flowing skies.

Janine Canan

Awakening

I
The world is a baby
wrapped in the gauzy fog.
Waves lap the shore,
a million tender voices babbling.
Afar, the lonely horn booms.

II
Walking past the house,
a brown-haired girl pulls on her gloves.
Frost hovers
on the roseless hedge.
Mercury streetlamps stain morning pink.
Crows tumble onto the pearly grass.

III
Waves shrug their shoulders
against the sand.
A lone gull stands on a boulder
sunk deep in the strait.
The sky is a magnificence
of blues and grays and whites.
Bent over the bluff,
an old fir waits for the wind.
Tentative raindrops stroke my face.
And the gull cries—

IV
Crows stomp the roof.
Morning stretches all the way to night—
third eye flaring.
All the birds have come to praise.
Cars, insecure, territorial, growl back.
Cows bury their noses in the endless lawn
where dreams are woven.
And Baby Moon plays peek-a-boo
in the palace of the fir.

Sophia at the Shore

Panting in her thick white coat
ruffled by the churning wind,
she watches gulls dart across the sand.

Turning to see me near,
she licks her shiny black lip
with her long pink tongue, and sighs.

As the waves roll in
under the cloudy blue dome,
she lays down her nose and offers herself to Life.

Jay Joy

Blue jay is back,
shaking his shiny black crest,

climbing the fir tree branch by branch,
past the confident crow

all the way to the radiant crown—
where he leaps in pure blue light.

Janine Canan

Knowledge II

What do the flowers,
lithe dancers in the light,
know of the stem—

to them the hairy hardy
water-bearer below
seems primitive.

But beyond their bright silk flags
lies a land
more splendorous still.

Reflection

The sun dives under the clouds
and mountains dim their snowy peaks.

Firs stare into the glassy lake—
where sky smolders on.

A gray mist moves
through the pondering trees.

An airplane hums human history.
And ducks fly toward the rosy north.

Beyond north—thought cannot go.
There in perfection lies the Sleeping One,

eyebrow arched above her lowered lid,
upon her mouth a blissful smile.

Awake in her dream, I look around—

Heavenly Play

To Toni & Helen

On the mountaintop
two women,
passing binoculars,
gawk delight
at two shiny ravens
squawking raucously
over the reeling
piney valley.

Shameless James

To James Broughton

James O James,
soon you'll no longer play
in the rain—
you who blissfully lay
with the sweet sugar cane.

James O James,
life is a game
beyond every frame.
The end is only a way
of beginning again.

Great Blue

Soon I will fly away like the great blue heron,
strong wings rowing the great blue sky.

Soon I will fly away like the great blue heron,
small feet fading in the great blue sky.

Soon I will fly away like the great blue heron,
lone cry lingering in the great blue sky.

Soon I will fly away like the great blue heron,
rising beyond the great blue sky.

Apple Orchard

To Don Shakow

Now that the apple orchard is inside you,
you can rest.

Now that the apple orchard is inside you,
you can let go of death.

Now that the apple orchard is inside you,
you are full of the sweetest fruit.

Bird Mother

Bird Mother,
You gave me your song.
You gave me your feathers.
You gave me your sweet nectar.
You gave me your nest in the eaves.

Bird Mother,
You greet me at the gate.
You show me the scaly pine's height.
You offer me the sky's vast freedom.
Now give me Your blessing, wherever I fly.

3   THE GOLDEN ARROW

At the Vulva Stone

The birds loudly love
the Goddess' ancient temple.
So do the pink daisies crowding the grass.

The sun pokes his tired old nose
through the clouds
to see Her grand and intimate stones.

A young man building muscle
jogs past the crevice
where Her child crowns.

And one wild sparrow lands,
rocking onto Her lush green mound,
drunkenly dancing.

Remembering

Hasn't tenderness the sweetest scent?
Haven't you missed mothering, and being sweetly adored?

We forgot something—was it God
the Mother who gave birth to all?

On the crescent moon She rocks her child through the night—
at dawn showering glorious sunshine.

Do you feel loved? If not, how uncover
that radiant jewel—open, aware, and free.

In this constant conversation of longing and loss,
we sing together in the light,

and our love rings unimpeded,
unending.....

Love, Enter

Love, enter this silence.
You alone bring light
to this dusty human drama.

To You I vow devotion,
to You I give my heart.
Love, let me take You fully in.

Let me become your Lady—
She who feeds the birds,
at whose feet the unicorn bows,

She who draws the most beautiful jewels
from the chest of the Earth
with the help of her friend, the rabbit and the fox,

She in whose face the monkey becomes sublime.
Let me serve You, Love,
My Only Desire.

Cluny Museum, Paris

A Poet's Journey

I was born chewing
on the spines
of my Mother's volcanic tits.

Shedding skins, cold
and embrous, I journeyed
through betrayal and love.

Surrendering into
Her molten Body, I entered
the heart of cosmic light.

Oh Mother

To Mata Amritanandamayi

Oh Mother,
You are so great.
Circling and singing, the swallows
come for Your blessing.

How can we,
Your children, find the way.
You are taking the world apart
and this chaos is awesome.

Still we are protected
by Your Love.
No matter how often we pull away,
You take us back.

We have so much sorrow—
it never stops flowing.
Dissolve our restlessness
in the beatitude of Your presence.

Open us
to the sky of Your love.
You dance with all the Gods—
heart-shattering is Your joy.

Let us fill from the well
of Your beauty.
Let us drink
from Your breast.

You are the sweetness
of the rose.
You are the full moon
in our hearts.

Kali Yuga

To Linda Johnsen

Through the hills of Her great burnt body
went my path, past creatures
penned and killed by men.
The night was brightly lit.
The roadside offered little shelter.
In the roaring cities no one was home,
and no child felt a mother's hand.

Into Her viney oaken hills I drove
ever deeper seeking love.
But the roads were concrete—
freeways zoomed with steel cages.
Harder and harder my heart pounded
until finally it broke.
You're not here! I cried.

I am everywhere, She answered.
In the clinging panicked oak,
the blooming prickly pear,
the hot red rose, rippling sweet scent,
the electric wire, listening stiffly.
I am in every light that flickers
on these glittery golden hills.

And I am in your yearning heart
that is opening into a temple.
So nestle deep into my moisty cave
where time never comes,
high up under my boundless heart.
There you will see the changing stars,
and I will bear you again and again.

Janine Canan

Stubborn Rose

Under the cedars the peacock wanders
searching—his scream floods the valley.
Under his long blue and gold tail
the grass turns emerald.

*

Day gapes
where the guardians used to stand—
elder- and blackberry, cedars, firs.
And night descends on the howling earth.

*

Painstakingly
the gray-haired woman
paints rose cream
upon her vanishing mouth.

*

Honored Heron on your rock,
can you tell me what o'clock?
Is it time to hurry home, or may
I stop and watch you stare at Rome?

*

The pilot points—*There!*
And like a ladybug we rise
through thick azure dusk
up to Her whirling white eye.

*

Back and forth, hummingbird struts
round the empty red feeder—
green opals buzzing
in the sun.

*

Stubborn Rose,
against the punishing winds you push—
tearing your last pink bud
wide open to the light.

Flight

Clouds heaped like egg-whites, pinked by the western sun. Grand canyons of clouds on an endless slate-blue ocean. Golden rose cliffs tumble down to the sea, fade to dusky pink and gray. Airplane passengers, knowing conspirators, smile over expanding azure seas. At the horizon cloud banks veil our approach. Surging white clouds—racing messengers of light—rush forward like friends to greet us. And a mysterious swathe of peach-streaked sunlit being passes by. Scorching tower of dazzling light! Impenetrable solid gray is washed in a pink that dilutes and floods the whole sky.

Paradise opens upon an earthly landscape. Under fuchsia sky a wide aqua sea crests with foam, as we fly westward into light through time and life suffused with more and more glory—in a dream where civilization is imagination, and beauty becomes reality. Oh beauty, gateway to the Goddess realm, heart's finest dream, mauve known now. This fading dream offering diaphanous passage to where? Oh happiness, oh gratitude, dimming unto night. This pale evening in Cloudland, where sleeping hearts yearn on toward the East.

Night. Beauteous arm of Snow Queen rises slowly over the Arctic world. Cool night is coming. Where, where, pale place? Life, what are you? Dim blue vault, clouded seas, rose crest continuing. The Journey—onward, onward—space—clarity—vast stretches—obscurity—nowhere—enveloping—impatient—incertitude—no answer—never—all that was hoped—gone—continuing—coming—more—so plain—and fades. Little dreams of clouds scattered over the sea.

Mother long lost, millennial Mother—I'm flying home.

Janine Canan

Goddess in the Museum

Marble figurine of a woman.
Mycenean terracotta statuettes of a goddess
wearing a long skirt and a flat headdress.
Ivory seated figure (the swollen abdomen of the figurine
suggests pregnancy).
Terracotta busts of three female figures.
Bronze figure of a woman or goddess.
[Unlabelled].

Terracotta perfume-bottle in the form of a siren.
Terracotta female head.
Terracotta plaque showing a female figure.
Terracotta perfume bottle in the form of a woman's head.
Terracotta woman wearing a finely patterned garment.
Terracotta goddesses (these brightly painted figures
are thought to represent goddesses because of their
tall cylindrcal headdress).

Two terracotta plaques showing a woman or a goddess.
Fragmentary marble statuette of a woman
from the Temple of Artemis at Ephesus.
Head of a woman, or possibly a sphinx.
Head of a woman from a statue.
Bronze figure of a woman or goddess.
Faience figure of a swimming girl.
Terracotta statuettes of women,
one with a hare, the other with a dove.
Female bust.
Winged goddess with a gorgon's head,
wearing a split skirt and holding a bird in each hand.
Limestone statuette of the goddess Isis with child Horus.

Plate with seated sphinx.

Marble statue of kore (a girl) holding a bird in her left hand
and a fold of her dress in her right.
Terracotta model of two female figurines,
perhaps the goddesses Demeter and Persephone.
Terracotta figure of a goddess.
Terracotta figure of a seated woman.
Terracotta figure, goddess.
Bronze figure of a girl holding a flower.
Bronze figure of a woman holding a flower.
Terracotta figure of a goddess seated on a throne.

[Label removed.]
Terracotta bust holding an egg and a cock.
Idealized head from a statue of a woman.
Helmeted head from a statue of Athena.
Clay figurine of a protective spirit dressed in a fish cloak.
Figurine of a woman with a child—a fertility charm.
Figurine of a seated pregnant woman.
Pottery doll—concubine figure.

Terracotta figure of a woman holding a dove.
Terracotta figure of a woman seated on a throne,
holding a tightly wrapped baby.
Terracotta figure of a goddess seated on a throne.
Terracotta figure of a seated woman.
Terracotta figure of a woman wearing a sleeveless tunic.
Bronze figure of Athena.
Bronze mirror with a support in the form
of a female holding a bird.
Terrracotta figure of a woman.
Terracotta upper part of a woman.
Bronze mirror stand in the form of a girl.
Woman wearing peplos.

Nereid or Aura (personified breeze), beneath her a bird.
Nereid or Aura, beneath her a fish
leaping over the waves.

Janine Canan

House of the Vestal Virgins

Although the Vestals
have been covered now
in plastic bubble and wrapping paper,
ready to be portered to some museum—
one stone Virgin still stands tall,
head and shoulder gracefully draped,

stump of her upper arm pointing in mid-day sun
past Caesar and Mussolini's plaza,
hot plastic crackling in the breeze
that stirs round her feet—
here where Vesta Herself once
fluttered eternal in Her golden flame.

Now motionless the vulva pool,
stuffed thick with lily pads
and edged with ruffly pink roses,
reminds of that entrance where all arrive
and soon depart—even us,
the living priestesses of Her creation.

Our Dark Lady

Goddess of Flowers,
Blossom Plume in scarlet robes
and Heaven's blue shawl with feathers,
Bird Mother, Virgin,
Our Hazel, Our Olive, Our Oak, Our Road,
Onyx Lady, Ebony Lady
You who dwell in mountain, well, cave and forest
with Your bee, Your dove, Your hare and Your horse,

You who continually answer our prayers,
Oh Mother of Truth,
matron of sailors, healer of the sick,
helper in the crypt, hope for miracles,
Holy Mary, Madonna of Fire,
Lady of Light, of Victory, of the widening Milky Way,
Adorable Black One,
Adorable Brown One,

Dark Tara, Tas-Samra,
Blackest Lady of Loreto,
You of the water, the snow and the dew,
Almond-eyed Mother, Our Silence, Our Joy,
Our Sweet Star, Our Source,
Hear us now, Our Dark Lady,
Goddess of Flowers, in Your scarlet robes
and Heaven's blue shawl with feathers.

To Tara

Adaptation of Tibetan Prayer

Green golden Goddess,
who hears every cry,
who dispells every fear,
Your laughter defeats every enemy.

Ablaze, You sit in a garland of fire.
One stamp of Your foot
makes every mountain on earth tremble.
The whole universe revolves at your feet.

A golden crescent adorns your crown.
Your face is a thousand autumns.
Your head shines with the light of a million stars.
Your eyes are the sun and the moon.

Revelations at Thalheim

To Mother Meera

I lift my head and gaze into your eyes—
a thunderbolt without beginning or end
pierces my heart.

*

Waves of the Mother—
endless tenderness—
flood my lonely garden with shocking bliss.

*

What is there to fear
when your smile
embraces every imaginable universe.

*

Your eyes,
huge shining pools,
deepen with obsidian mysteries.

*

One look from your Kali eye
evacuates whole destinies
of wrong—instantly.

*

Ah, petal by petal,
You unfurl the flaring lotus
of my yearning heart.

Janine Canan

*

Soft as milk,
clear as a mirror,
You are nearer than my Self.

*

Your eyes are golden
suns that pulsate not *No,*
but *Yes! Yes! Yes!*

*

You torch
the stubborn shell
around my seedling Self.

*

Your glance of honey
pulling me
into a web of incandescent love.

*

You are the golden lotus,
your petals woven from a million suns
blazing within.

*

Bubbling and gurgling,
my heart pours joy—
You are always here.

Janine Canan

A Child's Prayers

Oh Ma, Your breath whips wildly
through my crazy heart.
Blow, Mother Kali, all the ruins
from my dusty heart.

*

Open Your million gates.
Flood me with beauty.
Drown me in Your heart's heart.
Radiate me with bliss.

*

Soften my heart.
Stir till it turns to candy.
Melt to a thick sweet syrup.
And then, oh my Mother, drink me.

*

I am Your drop.
I am Your grain.
I am Your smallest servant.
Take me.

*

Vast Ocean,
how many precious jewels
have You sucked back
into Your boundless waves.

*

The moon
gyrates in ecstasy.
Flames leap up in joy.
At Your feet, multitudes fall in love.

*

I am Your lotus—I wave in Your pulsing breath.
All my petals open to Your brilliant light.
Joy enters my welcoming heart.
All my petals rise, crying Your name.

*

Mother, may I love
Your Creation, always changing.
May I love and let go.
May I love You only—everywhere.

*

I am the hummingbird
flying into the window.
Take me, Holy Mother, in Your loving hands.
Release me into the dazzling sky.

*

Oh
my Mother,
now we are
One.

In Your Miracle

Alone in the aqua-blue water
of Your body,
I whirl my prayer of love.

Green rocks greet me,
and greeny red fish swim by.
As I float on Your liquid bliss skin,
above me Your umbrella of light,

I am Your starfish daughter,
in Your undulating clear blue belly,
in the aquamarine of Your heart.

Lovers Quarrel

You were earth
and I was water.

You were abundant
and I danced over You.

When You disappeared
I grew deep,
dark as mystery.

Our Mother

To Alma Villanueva

Whoever loves us most
is Our Mother.

A million diamonds sparkling on the sea—
each one Our Mother.

Whoever, whatever
gives us light for our way—

is She not everywhere?
Our beautiful sinuous shimmering

Mother—
how She loves us.

The Golden Arrow

It lasts only a short time, this body;

time itself is nothing but imagination.

Love is the truth that cuts through all the dimensions,

an arrow flickering gold.

Love is the river that flows from one heart to the next

on its way to the ocean.

Love is the whole landscape

in every light.

Love is the voice, the gaze, the kiss of beings

practicing to be gods.

 # Notes

Page 23: Quotation is from Virginia Woolf's novel *Three Guineas*. (Harcourt Brace, New York, 1938).

Page 39: Ukrainian poet Anna Akhmatova (1889—1966) took the name Akhmatova from her Tartar grandmother. The quotation is the epigraph to her monumental poem "Requiem", composed during her son's imprisonment under the Stalin Terror, burned with the rest of her poems, memorized by a group of her friends, and published for the first time in Germany, 1963. Her poetry has been translated into English by D. M. Thomas (from whom I quote), Richard McKane, Stanley Kunitz, Jane Kenyon; and by Judith Hemschemeyer in an annotated illustrated two-volume bilingual *Complete Poems of Anna Akhmatova*.

Pages 49 and 63: "Erotic" ("Erotique") and "Your Name" ("Ton Nom") are from *Les Charité d'Alcippe* (Gallimard, France, 1956/1984) by Marguerite Yourcenar.

Pages 50 and 71: "Fourteenth Elegy" ("Elégie quatorzième") and "Prayer to Love Sorrow" ("Prière pour aimer la douleur") are from *Le Deuil des primevères* (Gallimard, France, 1901/1967) by Francis Jammes.

Page 77: "Whenever New Hearts Break" ("Wenn Junge Herzen Brechen") is from *Gedichte* (Reclam, Stuttgart, 1965) by Heinrich Heine.

Page 93: "Mirabeau Bridge" ("Le Pont Mirabeau") is from *Alcools* (Gallimard, France, 1920) by Guillaume Apollinaire.

Pages 94 and 111: "Love" and "Indestructible" are recreations of two of A. J. Alston's translations of the sixteenth-century Rhajastani Indian poet-saint Mirabai, *The Devotional Poems of Mirabai* (Motilal Banarsidass, Delhi, 1980).

Page 101: "Changing Woman, A Navajo Story Retold" is derived from a variety of sources, including Kathleen Jenks' "Changing Woman: A Therapist Goddess" (*Psychological Perspectives*, Los Angeles, Fall 1986); Hasteen Klah's and Mary Wheelwright's *Navajo Creation Myth*; Margaret Link's *The Pollen Path, A Collection of Navajo Myths*; Sheila Moon's *A Magic Dwells: A Poetic and Psychological Study of the Navajo Creation Myth* and *Changing Woman's Sisters*; and Gladys Reichard's *Navajo Religion: A Study of Symbolism*.

Page 113: "Stars on Fire" ("Les Astres") is from *Poèmes* (Gallimard, France, 1968) by Simone Weil.

Page 115: "Mira and Krishna" is the story of a sixteenth-century Indian queen who became the singing poet Mirabai, and wandered India in search of her beloved Krishna, the God of Love. Based on Mirabai's poems and A. J. Alston's biographical introduction to *The Devotional Poems of Mirabai*.

Page 140: This poem is a contemplation on the meaning of the words *A Mon Seul Desir*, inscribed on the Lady's tent in one of the Unicorn Tapestries displayed at the Cluny Museum in Paris.

Page 143: *Kali Yuga* is a Sanskrit term which refers to the present Dark Age of Materialism. It means, literally, "Kali's Yoke", Kali being the male demigod who presides over the fourth and most decadent of the four Hindu ages, the Kali Yuga (not to be confused with the Goddess Kali, addressed in "Oh Kali" and referred to in "Revelations at Thalheim").

Janine Canan

is the author of eight collections of poetry. Her work has been widely anthole gized. She has translated a volume of poetry by Else Lasker-Schüler, edited poetry collection by Lynn Lonidier, and compiled an award-winning antholog *She Rises like the Sun: Invocations of the Goddess by Contemporary America Women Poets.* Dr. Canan, a Stanford and NYU School of Medicine graduate, also a psychiatrist. She resides in Sonoma, California.

Praise for Other Books by Janine Canan

The Hunger "Distinguished poems."—James Laughlin, New Directions Pres

Who Buried the Breast of Dreams "Absolutely excellent!"—David Meltze author of *Arrows*

Shapes of Self "Told with that lulling incantatory charm of the Arabia Nights, a joyous and lusty book."—Andrei Codrescu, *Baltimore Su* "Remarkable—searing—portraits. A perceptive writer. Original, too." —Els Gidlow, author of *Elsa.*

Her Magnificent Body: Selected Poems "Whether naturalist, surrealist, myth ic or imagistic, the finely attuned sense Janine Canan displays of the inn relation between self and the other has made her unique in the art of verb portraiture."—Gary Gach, *San Francisco Review of Books*

She Rises like the Sun: Invocations of the Goddess by Contemporary America Women Poets—Recipient of the 1990 Susan Koppelman Award. "One of t best books to come from the Women's Spirituality Movement." —*Booklist*